GOOD ✦ OLD ✦ DAYS

WE MADE THIS
COUNTRY GREAT™

Edited by Ken and Janice Tate

HOUSE of
WHITE
BIRCHES
PUBLISHERS
SINCE 1947

We Made This Country Great™

Editors: Ken and Janice Tate

Managing Editor: Barb Sprunger

Associate Editor: Kelly Keim

Editorial Assistant: Joanne Neuenschwander

Copy Editors: Nicki Lehman,
Mary Martin, Läna Schurb

Assistant Editors: Marla Freeman,
Lisa Fosnaugh, Marj Morgan

Publication Coordinators: Tanya Turner

Production Coordinator: Brenda Gallmeyer

Graphic Arts Supervisor: Ronda Bechinski

Design/Production Artist: Erin Augsburger

Cover Design: Jessi Butler

Traffic Coordinator: Sandra Beres

Production Assistants: Janet Bowers, Chad Tate

Photography: Jeff Chilcote, Tammy Christian,
Kelly Heydinger, Justin P. Wiard

Photography Assistant: Linda Quinlan

Publishers: Carl H. Muselman, Arthur K. Muselman

Chief Executive Officer: John Robinson

Publishing Marketing Director: David McKee

Book Marketing Manager: Craig Scott

Product Development Director: Vivian Rothe

Publishing Services Manager: Brenda Wendling

Printed in the United States of America

First Printing: 2002

Library of Congress Number: 2001089861

ISBN: 1-882138-83-X

Customer Service: (800) 829-5865

Every effort has been made to ensure the accuracy of the material
in this book. However, the publisher is not responsible for
research errors or typographical mistakes in this publication.
We would like to thank the following
for the art prints used in this book:

Apple Creek Publishing: *Friendly Rivals* by Charles Freitag,
pages 32 and 33. For information on fine-art prints, contact Apple
Creek Publishing, Hiawatha, IA 52233, (800) 662-1707.

Jim Daly: *A New Beginning* by Jim Daly, page 9; *Territorial
Rights* by Jim Daly, pages 110 and 111; *All Lines Busy* by
Jim Daly, page 122; and *Radio Daze* by Jim Daly, page 126.
For information on fine-art prints, contact Jim Daly,
Eugene, OR, 97402, caroledaly@earthlink.net.

Mill Pond Press: *Continuous Vaudeville* by Jess Hager,
page 13; *Grandma Buck's House* by Luke Buck, pages 16
and 17; *Bridgeton 2* by Luke Buck, pages 4, 46 and 47; *Winter
Gathering* by Jess Hager, pages 60 and 61; *Incline Connection*
by Jess Hager, pages 82 and 83; *Rainy Night, City Street* by
Jess Hager, pages 4, 106 and 107; and *The Editor* by John Seerey-
Lester, pages 134 and 135. For information on fine-art prints,
contact Mill Pond Press, Venice, FL 34292, (800) 535-0331.

Paducah Flood-Wall Murals: *Grand Propeller* by Robert Dafford,
pages 5, 38 and 39; *1912 Port of Paducah* by Robert Dafford, pages
92 and 93; and *A Century of the Telephone* by Robert Dafford, pages
118–121. For information, contact Paducah-McCracken Co. Visitors
Bureau, P.O. Box 90, Paducah, KY 42002, (800) 723-8224.

Portsmouth Flood-Wall Murals: *Portsmouth Train Station* by
Robert Dafford, pages 26 and 27; and *Molten Iron Being Poured*
by Robert Dafford, page 72. For more information, contact
Portsmouth Murals Inc., Portsmouth, OH 45662, (740) 353-7757.

Printed by permission of the Norman Rockwell Family Trust. *Mr. &
Mrs. Henry Ford in the Old Shop* by Norman Rockwell, front cover and
page 84; and *Rosie the Riveter* by Norman Rockwell, pages 5 and 155.

Wild Wings Inc.: *Heartland* by Hal Sutherland, pages 4, 6 and 7; *The
Journey* by Hal Sutherland, pages 20 and 21; and *The Royal Hudson* by
Art Anderson, pages 5, 102 and 103. For information on fine-art prints,
contact Wild Wings Inc., Lake City, MN 55041, (800) 445-4833.

Dear Friends of the Good Old Days,

What is it that makes a country great? Every philosopher, historian, sociologist and politician since civilization began has tried to answer that question.

As we began to put together this special collection of memories, I posed the question to my wife Janice. "What made this country great?"

Janice always has had a knack of being able to sum up the most complicated of concepts in the simplest of terms.

"A great nation," she said, "must be blessed by God with a great land and great people."

She is so right.

America has been blessed with some of the greatest natural resources on Earth. Our rich, fertile plains feed our nation—and others as well. Our rivers move people and products. Our mountains, indeed, are both purple and majestic, but also provide precious metals, lead and coal. Woodlands give us lumber for our homes; bountiful orchards provide fruit for our tables.

But our greatest natural resource has always been our people.

Courageous, adventurous, faithful and indomitable—Americans are this and more. We are brash and bold, steady and strong. It is in our blood, our heritage and our history from Plymouth Rock to Tranquility Base.

Hundreds of volumes have been written about the famous names of American greatness. But what about the common and not-so-common folks who are the backbone of this great country? These are their stories.

From Ellis Island to the Oklahoma land rush—these are their stories. From laying concrete and asphalt to stringing rural electric lines—these are their stories. From the helm of a steamship to the engine cab of a train, from oil fields to wheat fields—these are their stories.

The "Greatest Generation"—the generation which cut its teeth on the Great Depression and came of age in time to fight and win World War II—was tried in the crucible of adversity and proved its mettle.

This collection of stories will touch you as those who made this country great share their memories of those days.

Go back to the time when the pioneering spirit was still alive from sea to shining sea. Return with them to the CCC camps, building roads and sending meager checks back home. Share news of good times and bad times with neighbors over that newfangled contraption called a telephone. Remember what it was like when radio and television were both in their infancy.

What made this country great? The answer is simple. It was our parents and grandparents, our husbands and wives, our brothers and sisters. It was you and me. We made this country great.

Ken Tate

Contents

• Moving a Nation • 82

• Informing a Nation • 110

• Inspiring a Nation • 134

Pioneering a Nation

Chapter One

★ ★ ★ ★ ★

*I*t takes a lot to make a nation great.

It first takes the greatest of natural resources, from fertile plains to verdant forests to rich minerals to abundant water. It takes virtually impregnable natural boundaries, from sea to sea and from desert to mountains.

Most importantly, it takes courageous people. Courageous people seek freedom for the sake of their heirs. They seek prosperity. They seek hope. Courageous people leave behind kith and kin and the comfort of home, braving all manner of tempests, danger and despair in hopes of finding a better life.

It was those courageous pioneers who stepped through the doors at Ellis Island. They took the toughest jobs in the cities, saving money in hopes of bringing wives and sweethearts, parents and siblings to this New World they now called home.

These same pioneers often moved westward, chinking together log homes or cutting sod bricks from the prairie floor. Whether they were pioneering in the suffrage movement, helping cut a farm from the Cherokee Strip, or just keeping together a family in the toughest of times, they kept hope alive.

In this chapter you will read the true stories of extraordinarily ordinary folks, courageous pioneers who—like millions of others—made this country great.

—*Ken Tate*

The Momentous Journey

Give me your tired, your poor,
Your huddled masses yearning to breathe free,
The wretched refuse of your teaming shore.
Send these, the homeless, tempest-tost to me.
I lift my lamp beside the golden door!

—*Emma Lazarus*

By Renie Szilak Burghardt

Though many years have passed since that momentous journey, my memory of it is still vivid.

I boarded the Navy ship General Stewart in the port of Bremen, Germany, with my grandparents (who raised me) and hundreds of other immigrants lucky enough to be going to America. Our arms ached from all the required shots, but our hopes and dreams soared on that September day in 1951.

Once aboard, women and children were ushered to one area, and men and older boys to another. Grandpa, of course, went with the men. Then we were assigned beds. I got an upper bunk and Grandma got a lower.

After settling in with our meager belongings—a few items of clothing—Grandma and I went up on deck, where Grandpa was already waiting for us. As the ship pulled out, a band on shore played *Auf Wiedersehn ('Til We Meet Again)*. Many on board had tears in their eyes. As I studied my grandparents' faces, their eyes revealed the bittersweet feeling I shared. We all knew that we would never see our homeland, Hungary, again. World War II had changed our lives forever; we were "displaced persons," refugees. But we were on our way to America, the land of new opportunity!

We had heard so much about America from friends and relatives who had gone before us. I had even begun to study English two years before our departure, though my command of it was still poor.

Our Atlantic crossing took 10 days, most in stormy seas. My grandmother was seasick most of the time, but I thrived and soon made some new friends. Dave, a young man who worked in the kitchen, brought me my first Coke, a new taste delight, and asked where I was going in America.

"I go to India," I told him.

He smiled and said, "That's probably Indiana, not India. In-di-an-a," he emphasized. "You will like America," he said. I also picked up a new phrase from Dave, which I began to use quite frequently: "Okey-dokey." Yes, in America, everything would be okey-dokey.

"There she is! There she is! The Statue of Liberty!" I stared, mesmerized, at the vision of the lady with the torch magnificently rising out of the sea.

Most of the kids whiled away the hours playing games and watching Roy Rogers movies in the ship's large game room. But excitement was easy to find. Once, while a friend and I were sharing an easy chair, a large wave hit the ship, throwing the chair across the room, and sending us and everyone in its path scrambling for safety.

In the dining area we often had to hold onto our trays with one hand to keep them from sliding off. On deck, we watched porpoises play in the water. One day we even saw another ship. It turned out to be the Queen Elizabeth. We chugged past the white cliffs of Dover, too,

and sang "There'll be bluebirds over the White Cliffs of Dover … " in their honor. Someone in the game room had taught us the song.

Then, one morning before dawn, my grandmother awakened me. "Let's go up on deck. The lights of New York are visible in the distance!" she told me excitedly.

I gazed sleepily into the black distance, slowly entranced by the trillions of lights on the dark horizon. It looked like a fairyland. That was my first look at America!

Then, as dawn broke, someone shouted, "There she is! There she is! The Statue of Liberty!" I stared, mesmerized, at the vision of the lady with the torch magnificently rising out of the sea. From my vantage point, she seemed to raise her torch higher and higher over the skyline.

I was so overcome with emotion that it seemed I could actually hear her speak the famous words I had learned in English class: "Give me your tired, your poor, your huddled masses yearning to breathe free." And so that moment was etched in my memory as the most thrilling of my young life!

Later, as we pulled into the harbor, we heard music again—*The Star-Spangled Banner*, the beautiful national anthem of our new country. Once again, we had tears in our eyes. We had arrived in America! As we streamed off the ship, I was compelled to look back at Miss Liberty once more.

Now, so many years later, I tell my little granddaughter how lucky and proud I am to be a citizen of these United States of America. And I remind her how lucky she is to have been born here. ★

★ ★ ★ ★ ★ ★ ☆

Three Words

By Beatrice Drummond

Three words—which mean the world to me,
Whose contents reach from sea to sea,
We all help form her destiny—
"America, my home!"

This land was made for me and you
Whose emblem's the old "Red, White
     and Blue"
And to her, we should all be true—
"America, my home!"

Her shores have been a harbor strong
To those escaping from the wrong,
Her name inspiring many a song—
"America, my home!"

She has her faults, the same as we,
Yet still her merits we all can see,
And God help us always keep her free—
"America, my home!"

God help her always, as of old,
To ere remain as strong and bold
As the early settlers there foretold—
"America, my home!"

Her beauty is so rich and rare,
We see God's blessing everywhere!
And an eagle soaring through the air
Means, "America, my home!"

I would not live elsewhere on earth
Than in the land which gave me birth;
God help me always see her worth—
"America, my home!"

I thank You, God, for letting me
Live in this land of opportunity,
And precious words to me—these three—
"America, my home!"

Early Days in the Big Apple

By Lois Costomiris

My father, Sy Weinstein, told me many times the story of how he came to America, landing at Ellis Island amid thousands of gibbering people of all nationalities. The customs agents could never really understand what each man said his name was, and some had very long names, so they generally gave them names that sounded like what they *might* have said. As a result, some of them were fairly close and others not close at all. For a name like Popposki, the agent might say, "Your American name is now Poppit." Our name might have been Weinstein, or it might have been some Russian name that sounded like that. For this reason, many descendants of immigrants cannot trace their ancestors back further than their arrival in America.

Pa came from a place called Volyner, in Russia, a village very much like a ghetto where Jews had to live. Jews could not live in all areas of Russia. He came from a rural village populated by Jews, but governed by Russians. The residents were a totally repressed group. They weren't allowed to travel unless they had special papers.

Our family had a house with a straw roof back in Russia. I remember Pa saying that the cattle came right into the kitchen, and lived in his house! Everybody lived in one room. He had a bed in a niche above the stove to keep warm.

My grandmother had to raise six kids including my father. The only thing she could do was run an illegal saloon. She was a bootlegger, I'd tell my father, which he didn't appreciate!

But she didn't get into trouble. There was an understanding between her and the state officials. There were kickbacks. She served the Russian peasants who lived there, and they had vodka and herring. It was a small restaurant-saloon that served home-cooked meals. I get the feeling it was a very poor, pub-type place where the peasants used to come after a day's work in the fields.

My grandfather specialized in copper work, and he made stills so they could make their own moonshine. Maybe that's how she got into the business. She had a lot of contacts and she was an excellent cook. People came from all over for her specialties. She grew many of her own vegetables.

And whenever anyone got sick, they came to her. It seemed that she was the nucleus of the community.

When Czar Nicholas came into power in the 1890s, it really got bad. Everybody was drafted—old Jews, and essentially any boy who was at least 10 years old. It was a death sentence when a 10-year-old had to put on all the garb of a Russian soldier and do what they had to do. I guess Grandmother said to her 18-year-old son, my father, "It's time for you to get going."

Pa's brother didn't escape the army. He got drafted and spent several years in the army before he deserted, went over the border, eventually found his way into Cuba, and then to the United States.

My father emigrated legally, about 1890. He got to Rotterdam and from there, came by boat to New York. My father had a terrible time when he first arrived because he couldn't speak the language.

All the immigrants were told the same story: In New York, the streets were paved with gold.

All the immigrants were told the same story: In New York, the streets were paved with gold. They were shocked to find that they'd have to work very hard, and that conditions were bad. But they were still much better off than in the old country.

New arrivals looked up a relative from back home, or someone else they'd known from their hometown in Russia. "We're here!" they'd say, and their relatives or old neighbors would put them up for a couple of months, maybe a year.

These people were also having struggles—conditions weren't good—but they were an awful lot better off than in Russia.

My father and mother met in New York City on the Lower East Side, got married and moved to Brooklyn. At first Pa worked in a factory as a laborer, making $2–$3 a week. He made pots; it was typical sweatshop work. Pa went from one laborer's job to another before he went to work in a large dry-cleaning facility.

Their first apartment was a third-floor flat in the Williamsburg section of Brooklyn. They had two bedrooms, a kitchen and a bath, electricity, a gas stove and hot-water heat. The kitchen was the center of family life, the heart of the home. You ate there, studied there and entertained there.

We had relatives who lived behind the store and they came over once a week to take a bath because they didn't have a bathroom. It was very common then in New York to go to the "the baths," a centralized bathing facility. Once a week, all the working people bathed there. This was in 1910–1918.

When all these immigrants moved in, they moved in with each other. How in the world would they learn the language? They went to the public schools' evening courses that were strictly for immigrants. The very most important thing to them was to become assimilated, and not be called a "greenhorn." Pa learned his English there. He wrote very well, considering that he worked 60–70 hours a week!

Williamsburg was an interesting neighborhood with lots of first-generation immigrants—Italians, Russians, Poles—and they were all friends of mine, except on Jewish holidays! One other kid and I were the only Jewish kids in my class. When we stayed home for a Jewish holiday, the other kids were mad, and then we really got beat up!

There were ethnic conflicts all the time, and we got together for protection. Now they call them gangs; we called them "social athletic clubs."

Everybody rented. No one I knew owned a home, and no one had a car. If you had a vehicle, you either were very well off, or you were a gangster.

Six families lived in apartments on one floor, all denominations, and all protective of one another. When I was sick, my father went to a neighbor across the hall—the resident "witch doctor" who really knew folk medicine. She looked at me, then gave me half an onion with something on it.

When we kids were small, our mothers went out with us when we played. Ma sat on the stoop—the front stairs of the building. Each woman brought a chair down or sat on a wooden crate from the grocery store. They sat out there and talked while the kids played on the pavement or in the street (there were very few cars).

We played the typical kid games in the street. We played Chinese handball against the buildings. Another game used the four corners of an intersection; we kicked the can and ran from base to base. And we clamped tin cans onto our shoes and ran down the alleys. We sat on the stoops and played "Actors and Actresses," and we played in the schoolyard. Nobody had a bicycle. We were not deprived for want of things to do, and we didn't just wander around. We played checkers a lot!

The roof was basically our back yard. We used the roof like you would use your porch or patio. After going up another flight of steps inside, we opened a big metal door, and we were on the roof. And we could hop from roof to roof, because the apartment houses were attached. We could go all the way down the block from one roof to another, then down another stairway. We did that quite a bit when the janitor chased us! You can understand why mothers didn't allow their children on the roof until they were at least 10.

The janitor usually lived down in the basement, next to the furnace. Sometimes he had a family. Sometimes he would forget to give us heat. Then we'd bang on the pipes with a hammer.

In summertime we sat out on the fire escape. We even slept there when it was hot.

We had an icebox. Think of that iceman, carrying ice to everyone up all those flights, leaving a stream of water behind him. The pan under our icebox was always overflowing and full of bugs. Ma was always fighting bugs!

In wintertime we didn't have to buy ice. We'd get a wooden box that vegetables came in, then raise the window and nail the box outside. We put our food in that box.

There were back yards, too—cement ones—but we weren't allowed there. They were called "courts." There was a big pole there to which everybody attached their clotheslines. We had open space back there and could see the bridge.

We lived in a market district, across the street from a chicken market. Vendors sold produce from their carts. There was a lot of activity and it was interesting just to take a walk. When I walked down from my apartment, there were hundreds of vendors and people milling about.

I never missed going to the movies on Saturdays. Our parents sent us there with lunch and said, "Don't come back!" We went at noon and came home at 8 p.m. In between we watched a full double feature, a short, a comic cartoon, and a chapter in a serial. That was what kept us coming—*The Green Hornet!*

We got all of our dishes by going to the movies. Every time we went in, we got a piece of china— a plate, cup, saucer, whatever they were giving away that week. Different theaters had different china patterns, but we didn't care if they matched.

And my father went to the movies religiously on Sundays. He saw every Hopalong Cassidy film ever made. Gabby Hayes was also his favorite. Hop and Gabby could do no wrong!

There were about 20 movie theaters in my neighborhood within walking distance. When we played hooky from school, we went to the movies. They opened at 10 a.m.

Ma was a very good cook and housekeeper. Above all else, she wanted to become a U.S. citizen, but she couldn't read or write, neither English nor her native tongue. I spent months teaching her how to write her name. I was 9, and every day we worked together until she knew how to write her name. She eventually learned to speak very broken English.

My brother died when he was very young, and I lost my mother when I was 11. As I was growing up, she was becoming mentally disturbed. She got worse and worse until she finally had to be put away. She didn't recognize me when I went with Pa to visit her. This hurt. It was a very unpleasant time.

Mother lived for another nine years, getting worse all the time. I couldn't take it any more, but Pa continued to visit her every Sunday. He'd get on the trolley car with a little sandwich for her, and she always recognized him. He didn't miss a Sunday. I witnessed extraordinary devotion between those two. She was in her 50s when she died.

From age 11, I was on my own. Nobody was there to take care of me when I got home from school. I had to carry my own key.

Every summer I'd visit my uncle in Albany for three or four days. He had a *house*! By no means was it a big one, but it had trees. He had a plum tree in the back yard, and he just picked a plum and gave it to me! That was just unheard of! And the grass—well, in our neighborhood, grass was something you didn't step on.

I cried when I had to go back home. It was terrible to have to go back after even a short time living with cars, trees, lawns, all the nice things of life. But my sadness wore off after a while.

My parents almost never visited my school; it must have reminded them of government, or the czar. They wanted me to get a good education above all else, but they didn't want to get involved with anybody that looked like "an official."

We had a PTA, but it was for second-generation parents. Pa didn't even know what a PTA was. The only time I ever remember him going to school was once when we had an open house at night. He came. He liked it. And he went home, and that was it.

I went to a very good high school, one of the top schools in the city. I had to take a special test to get in. It was very, very competitive. We had football and basketball, but I didn't participate in many extra-curricular activities. We didn't go back to school for anything after 4 p.m. That cost money; it meant riding the subway. Dances, plays and concerts were held during the day.

Until recently, I never fully appreciated the difficulties—all the labors and hard times—my parents endured. It took a lot of guts for these people to come to America.

In later years, my father had it much easier. Although he never said so, I knew how much it meant to him that I had fulfilled his fondest dreams for me: getting a high-school education and attaining a very good position. ✩

Can You Read German?

By Bill Krueger

My grandparents were all born abroad. They arrived in this country as middle-aged couples with some young children still at home. Though they easily adapted to the New World, they did not obtain United States citizenship until they were approaching old age.

Many elderly couples in my hometown were enrolled in citizenship school with my grandparents back in the 1930s, often accompanied by grown sons and daughters.

Children who were under 18 at the time their parents were naturalized became citizens automatically, but this was seldom the case with my grandparents' generation. It was a difficult and confusing period for young and old alike, but it produced some anecdotes and incidents we laugh about now.

My dad, born in Germany, assumed his parents had become citizens shortly after their arrival in 1914. He was in his early 20s when he was shocked to learn they hadn't. He hadn't been out of high school too long, so he decided to skip citizenship school and take the examination immediately.

The examiner really gave him the works, knowing that he hadn't gone to citizenship classes. He plied him with many detailed questions about provisions in the U.S. Constitution, and the composition and functions of federal, state and local governments.

But Dad did well. In fact, he missed only one question. One of his sponsors was the rancher for whom he worked. He had been born and educated in the United States, but as he and my dad left the examination room, the rancher wiped the perspiration from his brow with his bandanna and remarked, "Boy, I'm sure glad he wasn't asking me those questions!"

> *Back then, applicants for citizenship had to demonstrate their ability to read and understand English.*

Back then, applicants for citizenship had to demonstrate their ability to read and understand English. Though this was no problem for Mom, Dad and others who had grown up here, it was a stumbling block for the older generation. It was particularly hard for the menfolk, who seldom left their farms and had little opportunity to learn another language.

There were tricks to crossing the language barrier, sometimes suggested by the instructors themselves. My dad's father couldn't read English well, no matter how hard he tried. The frustrated instructor finally advised him to leave his glasses at home on the day of the test and the examiner would excuse him. But being an old Prussian soldier who didn't sidestep the issues, he brought them anyway.

The instructor was dismayed, but offered him last-minute advice to continue reading no matter what. The examiner tried to interrupt several times to ask him what a certain word was, but Grandpa kept right on reading! "OK," the examiner said with resignation when he had finished.

But it was my mother's Uncle John who had the best approach. Before leaving home, he stuck a few pages from a German newspaper inside his vest. At the conclusion of his reading the examiner said, "Well, not so good!"

With a grin, Uncle John pulled out the newsprint and said, "OK, you read German!" He passed.

In many ways, my grandparents and their contemporaries were good citizens from the day they arrived, being law-abiding and God-fearing people. This is probably why the naturalization process was a little frustrating. They felt it was more important for their children than for them. But they were happy to be in this country and had no regrets. ☆

Depression Log Cabin

By the Rev. Rupert Sigurdsson

In 1932, my mother and step-father, Mr. and Mrs. O.C. Robinson, purchased Lot 7 of the Thelma Estate on Asbury Road, about 20 miles from Atlantic City, N.J. The price was $15 per acre, to be paid $5 down and $5 per month. Since this was during the Great Depression, the mortgage was probably paid only occasionally. The first year's taxes were less than $2.

Work on the land started when I was taken out there on Saturday mornings before my folks went to work. I was supposed to start clearing the land for a driveway and a house. I was 13 years old then and thought it was great fun. I took a bottle of water and a bag lunch, and sometimes a school friend came with me.

Early that summer we moved out to the property from Atlantic City. We lived in an old tent that leaked with every rain; sometimes I tried to light a campfire in the middle of the night to get dry. When the tent collapsed one night, we knew we had to build a temporary cabin before winter.

But first we needed a supply of water. We bought pipe, a well point, sledgehammer and pipe wrench from Sears, Roebuck & Co.—all the supplies we would need to put a well down in our sandy soil, or so we were told. I think the local residents must have enjoyed many a joke at our expense as we tried to put a well down with that equipment. Finally, one of them lent us a well-boring tool to dig down to first water, which was about 18 feet below the surface. After hours of banging the pipe down with the hammer, we finally hit a good supply of water from our pitcher pump at 40 feet. We also got a good supply of blisters.

That summer we built a small cabin about 12 feet square. We survived that first winter in it; I say "survived" because our only heat came from a small kerosene stove. The cabin was built of local pine and oak logs. We stuffed moss between the logs to keep the weather out.

My mother was able to get a job in Philadelphia and came home on weekends, leaving my stepfather money so we could keep working on the cabin.

The next job was cutting logs for the house and stripping the bark off them. A grove of tall, straight pines grew on the back portion of our land. After cutting some, we used our old 1926 Nash sedan to pull the trailer we'd made to haul the logs out of the woods. We piled the logs near our house site and spent hours stripping off the bark with an old drawknife.

Our "helpful" neighbors told us that the pine we were using wouldn't last 10 years. That house, however, is still standing.

During the winter and early spring of 1933, my stepfather and I built the kitchen, a bedroom and a closet that I used as a bedroom. All our work was completed with hand tools—an ax, hammer and log saw—and we used 8- and 10-inch nails to fasten the logs together.

The roof wood came from an old hotel that was being torn down in the inlet section of Atlantic City. We hauled it home on our trailer. After the roof was finished, we caulked between the logs with cement made with sand from our own land.

Finally the house was livable. We moved in and found it very comfortable after living in our little cabin.

The next year we built a small log pump house and installed a gasoline pump. Finally we had running water in the house. When electricity came to our road, we changed the pump to electric.

In 1934, we added a large dining room and a music room to the front of the house. The final section—a cellar, bathroom and extra bedroom—was added in 1939. During these years we also built four chicken houses, all of local logs.

It took a lot of hard work, but it was well worth it. My parents operated their farm for many years. ☆

A Little Less Than Plumb

By Ray D. Rains

While it was obviously written in Destiny's Book of Life that I would become a carpenter and eventually a conscientious builder of fine homes, that had little effect on my first artistic endeavor. I am referring to the very first house I built for Violet, my wife, and myself, a house we now recall with candid humor. But it was so endowed with love and affection that it has become known to us, our children and grandchildren as simply "The House a Little Less Than Plumb."

The birth of that memorable house goes back to the mid-1930s. To Violet's disappointment, its birth wasn't quick and painless, but rather slow and grueling, drawn out over a period of years. Between long hours of fevered argument, sullen fits of depression, and ungarnished candor, it was finally completed to Violet's satisfaction, but completed in a prolonged manner, so to speak.

I shall never forget the look on her face the day I came home and announced confidently that we would build our own house. Her expression bespoke a mixture of wavering hope, a shred of stark fear, doubt, and what later proved to be pure, unadulterated skepticism. But, being young and brave of heart—and apparently holding immeasurable love and respect for me—Violet put aside her personal sentiments, set her sails with mine and embarked on a strange, dark voyage over experience's broad sea.

To begin with, our greatest blessing came from the fact that we both came from truly poor families, and we had just weathered a devastating Depression. In light of that experience, we reasoned that while there were many modern conveniences being installed in homes of the day which were certainly comfortable, they were not absolute necessities. Working on a strict budget, we soon decided that the first such luxury to be eliminated from our plans was the bathroom.

What made this omission easy was the fact that the 2-acre piece Papa had donated to our cause sported an almost-new WPA outhouse, complete with concrete floor, varnished stool and wooden paper dispenser. And Mama reminded us that there was an oblong, galvanized washtub hanging in her wash house, which we could use for a bathtub.

We had done our best, and it was ours. There wasn't a straight wall in the four rooms with their windows askew.

So, believing firmly in that Depression-era proverb, "Anyone who endured the 1929 financial crisis can endure anything, come what may," we spent our last few dollars on lumber and nails.

It would be an outrageous lie to say everything went smoothly. There were at least a half-dozen stubborn confrontations daily, some of them so severe that I often swore that I might lay the project aside uncompleted. But whenever I made such fraudulent threats, Violet would grab a hammer and gingerly start driving nails, declaring that she would build the house by herself if she must. It wasn't long before I was convinced that with her determination, it was just possible she could do it.

We had worked on the house from the middle of July (after we had laid our crop by) until heavy killing frost had settled over the cotton and cornfields. Hurrying to tie up the few loose ends

before the first flurries of snow descended upon us, we accomplished our goal in the first week in November. That afternoon, satisfied we had beaten Mother Nature, we walked outside to admire our house before we moved in.

It wasn't much to look at, but we had done our best, and it was ours. There wasn't a straight wall in the four rooms with their windows askew. The front door dragged tiredly against the pine floor and the roof sagged in places that could have been remedied by proper ingenuity. Most depressing was the crooked flue that seemed to lean fearfully southward, away from the blustery north wind. To be quite frank, there wasn't a plumb or level object in the whole structure. But we were satisfied with it and, linking arms, we headed for my father's house, declaring that we would move into our very own house the next day.

For several years the house served its purpose quite well. In spite of the walls being out of plumb and the flue leaning precariously, it was the birthplace of our children, and with the birth of each, we added onto "The House a Little Less Than Plumb." Using the shallow knowledge I had acquired working as a carpenter, I added a wing to each end, and covered the original structure completely. Today it is not discernible that such a shameful piece of work ever existed in the old house.

As years passed, the town spread southwest, taking in our original 2 acres. We sold the house and moved a short distance up the block where we built another house. At the time, it never occurred to us that we were building within sight of so many cherished memories.

Thankful for the opportunity to grow old while I daily view the old house, I am always grateful for the knowledge and understanding I gathered while building those first four rooms. Through those heated arguments and moments of contention, Violet and I discovered the simplest formula for a harmonious coexistence. It was while we were building that first house that we learned that merely a soft touch, a meaningful glance seeking forgiveness, or a good-night kiss at bedtime wiped clean the slate, ready for a bright new day tomorrow. ☆

Our Claim on the Cherokee Strip

By Otto Dittner as told to his daughter, Clara Dittner Huffman

We pulled down on Caldwell Flats just north of the line to make the run into the Cherokee Strip. My father, Henry Dittner, several neighbors and I had come from Halstead, Kan. I was 15 years old.

The registration booth was set up 3 miles south of Caldwell, Kan. We registered and Dad's number was 5,300. The prairie had been burned off just south of the booth for as far as the eye could see.

The Cherokee Strip was 200 miles long east and west, 69 miles north and south. It was measured off into sections with four farms to a section. You could file on just one farm and could own other land.

We set up camp 3 miles behind the line. I stayed and looked after the camp and stock while the others were gone. The men sat around the campfire at night and sang German songs. I still remember most of them.

The whistle on the flour mill blew at midnight. It really scared me. The wind blew hard from the south, and I could see big whirlwinds long after dark.

On the morning of Sept. 16, the men gathered along the line, ready for the run. Dad went just 20 miles into Oklahoma before his horse gave out, so he turned back. One of our neighbors staked a claim so he left it and came on back to camp.

We then returned to Kansas, but the following spring we went back to Oklahoma and bought a relinquishment. This land was 5 miles south and 1 mile west of Nash, Okla. So in 1894, we finally came to the Cherokee Strip to live.

My dad bought a team of mules, a team of horses and two wagons for the trip. He built a shack on one of the wagons that held the furniture and bedding. This is where my folks slept. The other wagon, covered with

oilcloth, was filled with food and cooking things. My three small brothers and I also slept in it. We were very excited and looked forward to the trip.

We brought along 30 hens and a rooster in a coop fastened under the covered wagon. They supplied us with eggs on the way down. We also took our milk cow. We had very little money, and we knew we faced very hard times.

We left Halstead on April 8, 1894. It was 160 miles to our claim. Along the way, we camped along creeks and cooked over a camp-fire. We lived on bacon, bread and coffee most of the way. We all took turns riding and walking. We arrived at our claim just as the sun was going down on April 16. We made camp, tended the stock and went to bed, exhausted.

The next morning we set the shack on a foundation. Dad had fixed it so we could remove the running gears and lower it onto the foundation. With that, we had a ready-built house to live in! Then Dad made a trip to Krimlin to get shingles to replace the oilcloth. We left the chicken coop under the shack, which made a nice shelter for the chickens.

It was 160 miles to our claim. Along the way, we camped along creeks and cooked over a campfire. We lived on bacon, bread and coffee most of the way. We all took turns riding and walking.

In 1897 we built an adobe house on a sloping hill just south of our present home. We used the wagon and team to haul red clay to the building site. I stomped a mixture of clay, straw and water with my feet. Dad made a frame from footboards and stuffed it full of the clay mixture. Then he added a shingled roof and board floors, and we plastered the inside with gypsum. The house had a stairway that led to the attic, which was never finished. My brothers and I slept in the attic. It took us two months to build our home.

I helped Dad farm for 11 years. We had 100 acres of land, and I could plow 2 acres a day with our team. We raised corn, sorghum cane, castor beans and a patch of watermelons every year.

One spring evening I worked later than usual, plowing on the south 40. It was already dark when I finally unhitched the team and started for home. The dog growled and barked, and I couldn't understand why. When I got to the field the next morning, huge cougar tracks covered every one of my footprints all around the field.

Those early days on the Cherokee Strip were hard, but we had a very good life. ✯

Pioneer Days in the West

By Edith T. Johnson

My parents left their home near Peoria, Ill., in the spring of 1876 to take a claim in western Kansas, 14 miles from Ness City. My two brothers were born in the sod house on the claim. Its 3-foot-thick walls kept it cool in summer and warm in winter.

By the time I arrived in September 1885, a two-room frame addition was nestled next to the "soddie." I slept in a trundle bed that rolled under the large bed in daytime, thus freeing the room for another use.

My father drove freight wagons from Great Bend to Ness City. What set him apart from most drivers was that he never carried a bullwhip. When he drawled "Giddee-aap!" the heavily laden freight wagons lurched forward, drawn by four of my father's best horses— but it was the authority of his voice, not the crack of a bullwhip, that set them in motion. He was never in such a hurry that he would

not stop to kill any rattlesnake he saw, coiled and glistening in the morning sun. Using the spade he always carried with him, he waged a one-man crusade to rid the plains of rattlers.

While Father was away on one of his trips, Mother saw a prairie fire coming in our direction. Black smoke rose in billows and tongues of red flame shot heavenward. These violent, destructive prairie fires came with a roar that struck terror in the heart of every rancher.

My mother, a small, dark-haired lady of French descent, was equal to any emergency. Hurriedly hitching the team to the wagon with its ever-present barrel, Mother had my brothers and me sit in the bottom of the wagon. "Don't move—and hang on!" she commanded as she stood, whip in hand, keeping the horses on the dead run. The barrel bouncing, we fairly flew over the prairie toward the plowed furrows of the firebreak.

Once there, Mother hitched the horses to the sod-breaker; then, lines across her shoulders, she gripped the plow handles. I can still hear her excited voice as she urged on the horses while she ran, holding the plow in the ground to turn more of the lifesaving furrows. Soon some neighbors came, and through their combined efforts, our ranch was spared.

Many burned corn for fuel. At 10 cents a bushel, it was cheaper than shipping it. (We also gathered buffalo chips from the plains; stacked like bricks to dry and burn with coal, they made a quick, hot fire.) When Father kept missing corn from his crib, he knew pretty well where it was going. He hollowed out a couple of ears and put a little gunpowder in them.

Then he put them back in the crib where they would be handy.

A few days later, the Smith boys, 6-year-old twins, came over and blurted, "You ought to have seen our stove! It made the most terrible noise! The lids flew off! Pop yelled and burned his fingers when he was picking them up!" Needless to say, no more corn came up missing.

One day I was teasing our old boar, poking a stick through the fence. He was chomping and foaming at the mouth, no doubt contemplating what a tasty morsel I would make. But Mother saw my performance and gave me the spanking of my young career.

I loved it when Father read to us in the evenings. There was talk that someday people would fly. Mother was skeptical, but Father believed it implicitly. He was a dreamer and welcomed new ideas with open arms. He should have been a scientist.

As I listened, my enthusiasm grew. I figured that if people were going to fly, 5 years old was none too young to start. I decided to experiment a little on my own.

The folks had built a low cattle shelter, and some shingles were leftover. I selected two large ones; then I climbed up on the shed, tucked the shingles under my arms, flapped up and down a few times, and took off. I picked the low side; nevertheless, the ground seemed to come up so fast that I made contact in no light manner. I wasn't hurt badly but I was pretty well shaken up, and I could have used a little sympathy. But so close on the heels of the unfortunate episode with the hog, I felt my parents would not understand this astounding performance. So, in respect for my bottom, I kept that adventure to myself.

We were blessed with good health, and it's a good thing we were, as the nearest doctor was 50 miles away. My only acquaintance with medication was castor oil for the inside, and turpentine and lard for the outside, the latter lavishly applied to my chest, and then covered with flannel. After one round of this combination, we learned to stay well to escape the "cure."

My father decided to quit freighting and go into the cattle business. He borrowed money to buy 200 Texas longhorns. They were long-legged, lanky and wild, but Father was sure of a good profit from them. His dream never came true, for the market declined instead of going up—and we lost our ranch when we could not pay off the mortgage.

After we lost our ranch, Grandmother wrote for us to come to Delphos, Kan., in the eastern part of the state, where we could live on her farm. Hard as frontier life had been for Mother, she was reluctant to leave the ranch, for she had lived there for most of her life.

We stayed in Delphos with Grandmother until our new home on the farm had been vacated. After a few days, I turned 6. Grandmother gave me a party, and that enabled me to meet Goldie Davis. She had big blue eyes and long blond curls, and she wore many petticoats that made her dress bounce like a ballerina's tutu when she walked.

I was fascinated. I wanted to look, act and be like her. One day she brought over her pet cat dressed in doll clothes. When I reached in the buggy to pick him up, he gave me a wild look and streaked for home. He lost his dress on Aunt Kate's rosebush, but the hood stayed on, cocked over one ear as he glared back at us from his porch. Goldie, hands on her hips, looked disgustedly after him and exclaimed, "Well, the ----!"

I tried to emulate her just once too often. When I added some of her colorful words to my vocabulary, I was chastised so promptly and thoroughly that I dropped the whole thing like a hot potato. After that, my long, straight, brown hair seemed more endurable.

I was glad when Father told us that the former tenants had moved out of our house and we could go to the farm the next day.

Our new home consisted of a large house and 160 acres along the Solomon River valley, with lots of trees, a large apple orchard and a row of peach trees. To this day, no peach has the flavor those peaches had.

Everyone was busy; life was different and good. We arrived in the fall, when fruit was abundant. One evening several neighbors came over, bringing their favorite paring knives. They said they were there for an "apple-peelin" to make apple butter the next day. When we'd peeled enough apples to fill our outdoor kettle, Mother put sorghum molasses on to boil. When it threaded from a spoon, she poured a plate for everyone. That was my first taffy pull.

We canned, dried and pickled everything for our winter's supply of food. A large platter of home-cured ham and buckwheat pancakes for breakfast sent us off to school in high gear. We had parties, spell-downs (or spelling bees) and box suppers at our country schoolhouse.

The girls decorated their boxes in pretty colored paper. The prettier the box, the more it would sell for. Some of the girls would tell their boyfriends what color their box was so that he would buy it and they could eat together. I'll admit that at that time, I still cared more about what food was in the box then who would buy it, but time changed that.

We attended church regularly. Once Father was taking off his overcoat and placed his hat behind Mother. When she sat down, there was a crunching noise. She had sat on his hat. Father's face got a little red as he retrieved his hat and poked it back into shape as best he could.

Four of my closest friends all had horses of their own. Soon I was willed a pony of uncertain age named Daisy. I was very proud and happy to have her. None of us had saddles; a blanket held on by a strap was sufficient.

The summer I was 12, Mother taught me to cook, make bread and bake pies. By fall I knew why. On Nov. 5, we laid her to rest in the Delphos Cemetery.

We raised lots of chickens. One rooster was a freak, devoid of feathers except on his neck. Come cold weather, I made him a wool suit coat and pants. I sewed his coat to his pants so he would not lose them. Erect, he swaggered over to show the chickens. They were frightened of him and scattered in every direction. Every time he approached, they ran. I ruined his social life.

Father tried everything in the book to stop a white leghorn hen from setting. Everything failed until I poked her tail feathers in the bluing bottle. She looked back, saw the tail, gave a squawk and started running. Every time she looked back and saw blue, she squawked and ran faster. Finally, exhausted, she lay there,

feet in the air, flaying the breeze; I guess she thought she was still running. I removed the offending feathers, and she never looked at another nest.

The winter I was 14, some of my friends came to go horseback riding. I took Prince, a high-spirited horse I was not supposed to ride. However, he behaved very well, except that he'd arch his neck and prance sideways down the road at the least excuse. We got along fine until my friend Bob said, "Let's see who can get to Bron's Pond first."

When we drew even, I kicked Prince in the ribs. That must have been what he was waiting for. He stretched those long legs as though he were enjoying the race. But he miscalculated, for instead of stopping at the edge of the pond, he turned short. I didn't, however, and I sailed ahead like a frog hunting for deep water.

The water wasn't deep where I landed, but it was breathtakingly cold. I tried without much success to enjoy my friends' hilarity as I sprawled there in the mud and water. Bob splashed in and helped me to dry land. Someone brought my horse up. They tried to help me mount, but dripping mud and water, I just wasn't Prince's type. Every time I tried to mount, he sashayed his rump away from me. Finally I had to exchange horses with Bob to ride home.

My father was furious with me for taking Prince. Exasperated, he exclaimed, "Edith, I have tried to be a mother as well as father to you ever since your mother died, but I guess I've failed!" At that point, I collapsed in his arms.

Later I found myself in bed. Soon our good friends, Dr. and Mrs. King, were there. Doc patted my arm and said, "Now, now, you're going to be all right. Just shock. Mrs. King will stay with you tonight, and tomorrow you can try out that new sidesaddle your father has been saving for your birthday. On my way out, I'll tell the young man who has been waiting that he may come in."

I knew without being told that it was my loyal friend, Bob.

Those pioneering days on the prairie were filled with tough times, but we sure knew how to have fun, too. ✩

★★★★★★★

What Would Grandma Say?

By Naomi Richwine

With modern women occupying key positions in all trades and professions, it is hard to realize that it was not all that long ago that their demands for full suffrage finally became a reality.

My mother, Louisa, and her sister, Sophia, were known and ridiculed in our little town for their radical views in regard to the role of "the weaker sex." They had been advocates of women's suffrage for a long time. They had been voting in city and school elections for years, so in 1920, when the 19th Amendment offered them full suffrage, they could hardly wait to get to the polls. But Grandma made it plain that she did not approve of this tomfoolery.

The day they voted for the first time in a presidential election was a red-letter day in our family. Although the two women had been thoroughly coached by their husbands, they were excited beyond restraint as they took off for the polls. It was the culmination of plans that had simmered in their minds for months.

Daddy gave Mother a few last-minute admonitions. Having voted earlier in the day, he had visited the polls at intervals during the morning to keep tabs on the extent of feminine participation. There was a great deal of conjecture as to whether or not the women would actually seize their long-coveted privilege and, if they did, whether it would make any difference in the election's outcome. It generally was assumed—particularly by men—that wives would vote as their husbands advised.

"Don't let it worry you," he summed it all up. "You may get to cast the 100th vote. They were up to 96 the last I heard.

"Just remember what party you're supporting," he added as he closed the door behind them.

Grandma was baking bread that day, and as they left the house, she turned out the dough for kneading.

"Silly women," she mumbled as she gave the dough a savage punch. "Women don't know anything about politics. They'd better stay home"—another punch—"and tend to their own business."

That evening, the women's adventure at the polls was the topic of conversation. Louisa and Sophia had defied convention and gone clear up to the lion's mouth and they had voted. And they'd voted the way they wanted to!

"What good did it do them to vote?" Grandma grumbled over her knitting. "What is the world coming to anyway? Women trying to tell the men how to run things when they should be at home cooking meals! The girls made fools of themselves today!" she exploded, raising her voice an octave. "Next thing we know, they'll be drinking whiskey and wanting to go into the pool hall!"

Times have certainly changed since that day long ago. I'm older now than Grandma was that memorable day when the women first exercised their right to vote. And I've seen women serve as lawyers, doctors and prime ministers, as well as plumbers, congresswomen and preachers. All I can say is that wherever she is, Grandma must really be pounding the dough! ✶

The pagoda-style Portsmouth, Ohio, train station as it appeared at the turn of the 20th century, sat between the N&W and B&O tracks. The wood-burning engine on the tracks belonged to one of the many short lines running in southern Ohio during the mid-1800s. This mural by artist Robert Dafford was painted on the Portsmouth flood wall in 1999.

I Remember Casey Jones

By Georgia Wissmiller

I knew Casey Jones well. He was my father. No, he was not the Casey Jones immortalized by the well-known railroad ballad. He was, however, a locomotive engineer—one of the best. His given name was Clarence George Jones. That he should acquire the name of "Casey" Jones at the start of his railroading career seemed natural and inevitable.

Many years have passed since Casey climbed into the cab of a Pere Marquette locomotive at the Eighth Street yard in Saginaw, Mich. Time and progress have wrought many changes, forcing those glorious days swiftly into a dim past.

Powerful diesel engines now occupy the rails where once the steam locomotive proudly stood. The old Pere Marquette railroad Casey knew and loved no longer runs tirelessly through the state of Michigan. Gone also is Casey Jones himself, the faithful old pioneer who guided the mighty "iron horse" over a span of 42 years. Were it not for the wonderful gift of memory, those days would be forever lost. But in moments of quiet reflection they return, flooding my mind with happy thoughts of days long past.

There were three children in the Jones household, a son and two daughters. I was the baby sister, born in 1920. Mother, then 36, noted a sprinkling of gray in her long, dark hair. Her once-slender form had yielded to a well-rounded matronly figure. Sparkling blue eyes accented her pretty face.

Time had rendered a few changes in Casey, also. His luxuriant crop of wavy hair had diminished to a small island of fuzz atop his head, bordered by a row of fringe above his collar. He was a broad-shouldered, stocky man. In his youth, Casey had proven his athletic ability on the gridiron and baseball diamond. Now, at 42, he prided himself in keeping physically fit.

Father seldom missed a day of work. In the scorching heat of the summer sun, or the icy chill of a winter storm, Casey Jones was on the job.

Mother and Father were both born and raised in the little village of Warren, Ind., in Huntington County. Each year Mother would use her railroad pass to visit the folks back home. Rarely did Father allow himself the luxury of a vacation trip. However, at Mother's insistence, he agreed to accompany us when I was about six months old. Naturally, I do not recall the events of that trip, but I never tired of hearing Mother relate the story.

Our journey began pleasantly enough. We boarded the train at the old Potter Street depot in Saginaw. Soon we were rolling out of the station on our way to Detroit, the first leg of our journey. Father disappeared into the smoker (a special coach for men, as women seldom smoked publicly in those days).

The train whistle was announcing our fast approach to Flint when an excited Casey burst through the narrow swinging doors separating the coaches. Hustling down the aisle to where Mother sat peacefully enjoying the scenery, he blurted, "Anna, guess what I went and done?"

Puzzled, Mother replied, "Why, I don't know. What did you do?"

"Darn the luck!" Casey sputtered, slamming his hat on the back of the seat. "I went off and left our baggage sitting on the platform in Saginaw."

"Well," Mother reasoned calmly, "we'll just get off at Flint and take the next train back home."

"We ain't a-gonna do no such thing!" Casey exclaimed. "I'll wire Saginaw to have our baggage sent on the next train."

So our journey continued. Mother was thankful my diapers and clothing were packed separately in a bag at her feet. This first experience of traveling with Father prepared Mother for future trips.

Since Father worked away from home much of the time, Mother assumed the task of raising the family. With patience, love and a keen sense of humor, she guided our daily living. And she instilled the deep religious convictions that governed her every thought and action in the minds of her children.

Our lives centered on school and church activities. On wintry evenings we gathered around the big, potbellied stove and read from the multitude of good books that lined our bookshelves. When the mellow chimes of the old grandfather clock signaled our bedtime, we knelt at Mother's knee for prayer, then streaked up the cold stairway to the warmth of our bed covers.

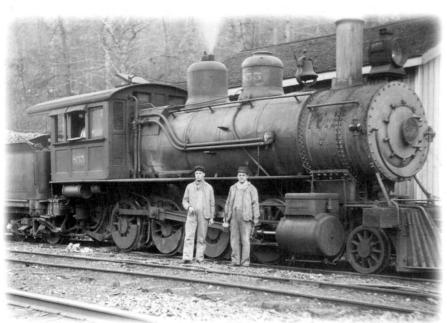

Our household usually maintained an atmosphere of tranquility. However, with one brief visit home, Father could drastically alter our peaceful existence.

I recall one particular evening when he arrived home unexpectedly. Mother was attending a missionary meeting at a neighbor's home. Father decided to meet Mother and escort her home, but as the meeting was still in progress and he didn't want to embarrass Mother by appearing in his grimy overalls, he was left no alternative but to wait outside.

He stood near a huge maple where he could observe the ladies as they left the meeting without exposing his presence. A neighbor became suspicious of his actions and called the police. In the glare of the policeman's flashlight, Father, flustered and indignant, struggled to answer the questions fired at him.

"What's your name," the officer barked, "and why are you hanging around here?"

Partially regaining his composure, Father retorted, "My name is Casey Jones and I'm waiting for my wife."

"Oh yeah?" the policeman sneered. "We'll see about that." He was then admitted to the house to verify Father's story.

Mother was blissfully unaware of the drama taking place outside. To the best of her knowledge, Father was on the job miles away. She was astonished when the officer summoned her onto the porch to identify her husband. Poor Casey! He seemed to possess a special talent for creating embarrassing situations.

Casey was a magnificent storyteller. An unusual memory coupled with a vivid imagination gained him many an appreciative audience. He also loved to argue. Mother vainly strove to divert his conversations from controversial subjects. But his timing was as perfect as that of the railroad watch he carried in his pocket on a long, gold chain. No sooner were our guests seated in the parlor than Casey would open the conversation with: "Now Anna ain't gonna like my saying this, but—" Boldly, he would launch into a lengthy oration of the forbidden subject while Mother sat by helplessly.

I cannot remember Father ever being sick in bed. He was, however, a firm advocate of the benefits of patent medicine. Faithfully he gulped down a variety of Indian herbs, bitters and teas that were constantly brewing in an assortment of Mother's fruit jars. Occasionally an ailment occurred which required a doctor's prescription. Then Father completely ignored the label stating the proper dosage and tipped the bottle for a healthy slug. It was his theory that if a tablespoon would bring relief, half the bottle would cure him—and twice as fast.

Mother would throw up her hands in despair. "Clarence Jones," she scolded, "if ever you do become seriously ill, no medicine in the world will help you, for you will be immune to all drugs!"

I shall never forget the day I nearly fell victim to Father's home remedies. I had been playing in my bare feet and cut my heel on broken glass. To my dismay, Mother had gone shopping, leaving me to the mercy of an eager father who insisted upon placing a strip of fat bacon on my wounded heel. Such a remedy was unknown to me. Terrified, I fled the house and ran screaming down the street. Close behind me raced Father, still clutching a huge slab of bacon and pleading, "Come on back here! I ain't gonna hurt ya!" How startled my poor mother was as she witnessed this scene on her return from town!

The climax of our summer vacation was a train trip, usually to Indiana to visit relatives. We arrived home from one such trip at 3 a.m. to find the house locked and the key missing from its usual hiding place. When efforts to pry open a downstairs window failed, Mother had no alternative but to wake a neighbor who gained entrance through an upstairs window with the use of a ladder. Once inside, we discovered that the windows had been nailed down and every dresser drawer securely locked.

I have never seen Mother so furious. When Father returned home a few days later, he explained that fear of a burglar had prompted his action.

"Clarence Jones," Mother admonished him severely, "if a burglar had entered this house, he would have felt certain that a fortune was locked in those drawers. Every stick of our furniture would have been smashed to bits."

"Oh, bosh!" Father grumbled as he stamped from the house.

Father seldom missed a day of work. In the scorching heat of the summer sun, or the icy chill of a winter storm, Casey Jones was on the job. He loved the life of a railroad man. Perhaps the thought of following the shiny rails stretching as far as the eye could see appealed to his restless nature.

Only once did Casey threaten to leave the railroad. In a grinding crash at a crossing, his engine had struck a car and the life of a young father was ended. Sick with sorrow, Casey slumped dejectedly over the kitchen table, his head in his hands. "I'll never run an engine again," he moaned. But he was wrong. Within eight hours, he reported at the caller's office.

Slowly, almost reluctantly, Casey climbed into the engine cab. He checked the instrument gauges before placing his hand on the throttle. Huge puffs of black coal smoke belched from the engine's stack, its pungent odor penetrating the night air. Casey felt the powerful surge of the engine as its gigantic wheels ground into motion with slow, convulsive lurches. Gradually the momentum increased until a steady, rhythmic clickity-clack filled his ears. Approaching a crossing, he sounded a shrill, incessant warning on the steam whistle. An endless ribbon of track unrolled before the powerful beam of the headlight as the engine sped onward through the black night. A quiet peace supplanted the turmoil within Casey's breast. This was his life; this was where he belonged.

At the age of 68, Casey retired. It was a joyous occasion, yet it bore a note of sadness. Transition to a life of leisure was difficult. Each day a magnetic force summoned him back to the railroad yard. But without his familiar blue-and-white striped overalls, long-billed cap and battered dinner pail, Casey no longer belonged amid the maze of steel tracks. He wandered aimlessly, a lost and lonely figure.

Shortly after celebrating their golden wedding anniversary, Mother's health began to fail. In December 1960, a severe heart attack took her from us. Three years later, at the age of 84, Casey joined his beloved wife. I visited him in the hospital as he lay close to death. He was tossing restlessly on his bed, muttering, "Got to keep the railroad running."

Yes, the railroads have changed since Casey Jones made his final run. The low, mournful wail of the freight train whistle no longer echoes across the countryside. Someday, a new mode of transportation may replace the railroad entirely, but of this I am certain: As long as trains run, the spirit of Casey Jones will forever abide happily in the cab of the engine. ☆

Courage

By Mary Noble

My husband's grand-mother was widowed at the age of 33 in the last decade of the 19th century and was left with a 10-year-old girl to bring up alone.

When Nellie and Earl married, they didn't go into farming as most young couples did, for Earl had learned the tinsmith trade. He worked for another man, making tin pails and buckets, and cooking utensils for sale in the tin shop. When the owner sold out, Earl was left without a job, so he went to a town 10 miles away to do the same work for another employer. Nellie and their daughter, Addie, stayed behind in Edwards while Earl boarded with his new employer in Fine. He came home only on weekends, when he could. Earl was not very strong; he had contracted consumption, now known as tuberculosis.

Earl walked the 10 miles to visit his wife and daughter. To go back on Sunday afternoon, they would hire a horse and buggy at the livery stable and drive halfway to Fine. From there, Earl would continue on foot while Nellie and Addie drove back home.

Even though the family was separated, they kept in touch by writing letters. In one letter Earl wrote that if he were well, it would be better if they could move, because of the expense of coming home to visit. He also sent 5 cents so Addie cold buy some peanuts.

In another letter, Earl mentioned a shirt that Nellie had made and sent him. He said it fit well but he didn't want another like it because he didn't like the way he looked in a dark shirt. He sent candy for Addie, but he didn't come home that weekend because he didn't feel like walking.

As in all the letters that have been preserved, the need for money is mentioned in the last one. Earl asked if wood had been delivered and if his wife and daughter were keeping warm. He wrote that he would send money for wood as soon as he could. This time he promised to send Addie some peanuts and toothpicks.

His health deteriorated rapidly after that. Soon there were no more letters and no more weekend visits. Earl died of the disease that had plagued him for so long, and Nellie and Addie were left alone.

If life had been hard before, it must have been even harder after that. Nellie took in washing and ironing to keep food on the table and pay the rent. Water had to be carried, then heated in the copper kettle on top of the wood-burning stove. Then she scrubbed the clothes by hand on a tin washboard and hung them outside to dry. She heated heavy flatirons on the stove and spent hours standing over the ironing board.

After a while, Nellie decided she and Addie needed a home of their own. She bought a piece of land at the edge of town and contracted to have a house built for $500. When it was ready, she and Addie moved in. Nellie kept right on with her work in order to make the house payment of $1.50 a week. By now, Addie was old enough to help with the work, so Nellie sometimes took in boarders. She also worked at the hotel, baking for New Year's and Fourth of July celebrations, and sometimes helped other women with their housework. All of these chores brought in enough money so that the house was finally paid for.

Many years later, Nellie sold that house for $1,500. She put the money in the bank. Soon thereafter, however, the Great Depression began. The bank failed, and Nellie lost 70 percent of her money. Addie had married by then, and had a daughter and a son of her own. Nellie worked for the local doctor for $8 a week.

Nellie always had to struggle to make ends meet, but she never went on welfare. She had good friends and neighbors who were always willing to help each other in times of need. They lived by the Golden Rule. ★

Friendly Rivals *is the title of this painting by artist Charles Freitag. The scene depicts good neighbors on two sides of a friendly tractor feud stopped for a short visit to the local Farmers' Cooperative. The red tractor in the foreground is a Farmall Model H; the green tractor is John Deere Model A.*

Old Iron Lives On

By Susan Peterson

Editor's Note: Pioneering this great nation would never have been possible without the advent of the small farm tractor. The Fordsons, Deeres and Cases that found their way into fields and valleys were in many ways pioneers in their own right.—KT

Even people like me—a mechanical ignoramus—can appreciate the rugged simplicity of the old John Deere 2-cylinder motor. And even though I was born long after Detroit ceased production of Henry's wonderful Model-T, I still enjoy the busy clatter of our 1925 1-ton Ford truck's motor.

Aficionados of "tired iron" seek out rusting wrecks in fields, old barns and back lots. They scour flea markets, junkyards and swap meets for parts, driving hundreds of miles on a tip for that hard-to-get magneto or transmission part.

There are specialists in antique outboards, cars, motorcycles and stationary engines, but in rural areas, a major subclass of tired-iron admirers is the antique-tractor buff who seeks out those small, old tractors like the Case, John Deere, Allis, International and Massey.

They were tough, those old tractors. The wife of a retired farmer, a neighbor of mine, remembers him driving an old Case back to the pond to fill up his sprayer. "He got a little too close," Betty recalled.

He threw off their little daughter who was along for the ride, and then jumped himself. "I was drying engine parts in my oven for a week," Betty said. Yet once the oil was changed, the fuel flushed and the magneto dried out, the old Case was ready to go back to work.

> *That tractor was a vast improvement over another family tractor, a rusty, worn-out Fordson. Cranking the Fordson gave my father plenty of cardiovascular exercise and lots of blisters.*

On my own family's weekend-hobby farm, we had a Model-C Case that rolled forth from its Racine, Wis., factory in 1935. Originally on steel wheels, ours had been rubberized for a better ride before we bought it. I remember road signs banning tractors with lugs (steel wheels) on paved roads—and steel wheels were the standard during World War II, when rubber was in short supply.

Old-time tractors have sturdy fenders and generous platforms for kids to perch on. A special treat was a ride home in the empty manure spreader.

I remember a tattered decal on our old tractor's fender that listed all the countries of the world in which Cases were working. It featured a proud bald eagle perched atop the globe, standing supreme above all, according to the J.I. Case Co. logo.

That tractor was a vast improvement over another family tractor, a rusty, worn-out Fordson. Cranking the Fordson gave my father plenty of cardiovascular exercise and lots of blisters.

Once during spring cleaning, a burning brush pile got out of hand on a breezy afternoon. My father decided to plow a firebreak to contain the fire, only to have the ever-faithless Fordson stall. It just sat there while the grass under it blazed away, the orange flames inches from the gas tank. It didn't blow up, but several people later expressed regret that it hadn't.

Part of the fascination with old iron revolves around the many ingenious ways farmers put it to work. Rigged with a belt pulley, a tractor could thrash grain, bale straw, cut wood and blow silage. Engines like the Hercules, Three Mule Team and Chore Boy pumped water, split

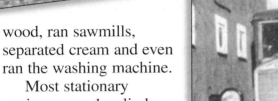

This old International 10/20 tractor was still running in the 1990s. (left).

The author stands between the family trucks. The Model T (right in photo) was still being used on the farm in 1991. (below).

wood, ran sawmills, separated cream and even ran the washing machine.

Most stationary engines were 1-cylinder "hit-or-miss" types with no-frills simplicity—no oil pump, distributor or starter, just the essentials of internal combustion with a cylinder and piston, igniter, crude timing device and governor, and a couple of oilers and grease cups for lubrication. For cooling the old make-and-breaks, a small open water reservoir mounted on top supplied the water jacket. The whole works was kept moving by a mammoth flywheel.

The farm of the 1920s and 1930s was still largely self-sufficient, though less so after the arrival of motors powered by fossil fuels. (After all, you couldn't grow a field of gas for the tractor the way you could oats for the team.)

Even though a tractor cost more to run than a team of horses, the cost was worth it. In 1890 it took nine man-hours to produce and harvest an acre of wheat and 15 hours to grow an acre of corn. After the tractor's arrival, the time was cut to four and five man-hours, respectively.

The earliest efforts to mechanize agriculture involved steam engines like the Fowler winding

drum engine and balance plow, which could turn 8 acres a day.

In the United States the age of steam lasted from 1880–1920. Steam tractor engines were mainly employed on the wheat farms of the prairies and far west, since they were too costly and heavy to use on the typical family farm.

Even early gas tractors were lumbering affairs, much like the 10-ton steamers they aimed to replace. One of the first gas-powered tractors to enjoy any commercial success was a bulky, single-cylinder tractor produced in 1902 by John Froelich, the granddaddy of countless "Poppin' Johnnies" to roll off John Deere's assembly lines.

Primitive gas engines at least had the advantage of not having a boiler of water to lug around. And they only needed one operator, unlike a steamer.

However, it took World War I to really put the small tractor to work on America's farms. Cropland in Europe was destroyed by the war,

Despite his short stature, Jean Peterson (author's brother) is actually driving this 1925 Ford truck on the family's hobby farm. The author notes that the pigeons have whitewashed the barn shingles.

and prices shot up as the demand for U.S. farm products soared. When so many farmhands went off to factories or joined the Army, rapid mechanization of the farm was inevitable.

Henry Ford's Fordson was small, relatively powerful, lightweight and cheap. They rolled off the famous Ford assembly line by the thousands in the 1920s. Curiously, my visits to old engine shows don't seem to turn up very many restored Fordsons. Instead there are John Deeres galore, a healthy number of Cases and Internationals and usually an old Rumley Oil Pull.

Most tractors of the 1920s and 1930s ran on economical fuels. Our Case C was designed to start on gasoline, then switch to kerosene.

The typical contemporary working small tractor is likely to be a compact, powerful diesel, which produces more bang for the buck and has largely driven the gas tractor out of the picture. Yet on smaller farms, you can still find post-World War I gas-powered Olivers, John Deeres and little blue-and-gray Fords.

The best place to see old tractors made young again is at meets for collectors of tired iron, which are usually held in summer. Exhibitors put their restorations to work, and engines running straw balers, lath makers and corn shellers give onlookers a glimpse of what farm life looked and sounded like in the 1930s.

The stark simplicity of the stationary engines and tractors introduced several generations of tinkerers to the complexities of internal combustion. Those backyard mechanics must find today's cryptic computerized cars frustrating.

My 1930 boat motor has an electric starter, but it also came with a crank, which I use once in a while just for the nostalgia of it. The cheerful chug-chug from my own past never fails to delight and satisfy. It's as if the spirits of now-departed engineers, mechanics and foundry workers are given a chance to speak again through the means of that durable, sturdy little motor. ☆

Invisible Legacy

By Willodean Rosenbaum

A legacy is usually a gift of money or personal property. But I believe we all leave many things to others, things that can't be seen with the naked eye. We may walk softly through life, yet we leave prints behind. It is entirely up to us whether we leave prints of kindness and love or gossip and hate.

My mother died when I was six days old. I was taken to live with my maternal grandparents on a small farm in Tennessee. We had no electricity or other modern conveniences. Times were hard. It wasn't easy to make a living in the 1930s and early 1940s. But memories of my childhood bring to mind Grandma's words: "We'll make do." That was the key to our survival.

Grandma was a tall woman. She wore her hair pulled up on the top of her head in a bun. She dressed in heavy shoes, cotton stockings, a long dress and a huge apron.

Grandma kept chickens. She carried the eggs to the little country store where she swapped them for sugar, flour, salt, soda and things we couldn't grow on the farm. She milked a cow, churned butter, worked in the fields, hoed corn and made a garden. She canned the vegetables we ate, fixed corn in brine, made sauerkraut in a churn, and dried apples.

Grandma baked huge blackberry and dewberry cobblers. I have never since tasted a pie that compares to the taste of those cobblers. She baked molasses sweet bread (gingerbread), molasses cookies, raisin pie and egg custard pie.

She made onion poultices and cough remedies, and brewed sassafras tea to help prevent colds and influenza. She created quilts from scraps of material left from sewing. Any usable part of worn clothing was used to make quilts. She could spin and knit, too.

Grandma did not complain about hardship; she simply found a way to make the most of what she had. She learned to draw satisfaction from simple things. She had little formal education, but she was wise; her ingenuity was phenomenal. She simply said, "We'll make do."

She cut old felt hats into strips and sewed them to the wick on the kerosene lamp so that all of the wick could be used. When there was no visible way, she found a way.

She was a quiet, shy woman in many ways. When we went to church, people often gave testimonies. Grandma usually remained quiet. Spoken words were not necessary. Her life was an example of her faith in God. She trusted Him to supply her needs, not her wants. She learned to cope with whatever came her way. She kept hope alive in her heart—hope that tomorrow would be better, hope that the crops would grow better next year, hope that there would be peace in the world.

She was an old-fashioned grandma. She didn't have money, but she had plenty of love to share.

She was tired from years of hard work. On a cool March day, just a month before my 13th birthday, Grandma went to her eternal reward. The only possession she left me was a patchwork quilt, pieced and quilted by her loving hands. But her invisible legacy to me is enormous.

The love she gave me has remained in my heart, and I have shared it with others. It has helped me through many dark days and it's always there when I need it most. Hope has stayed alive in my heart. My abiding faith in God keeps me going. The ability to "make do" has saved many a day for me.

It has been many years since Grandma's earthly life ended. I have shared the love, faith and hope Grandma shared with me with my own two children. Both are grown and married now, but both have learned to "make do" when necessary. I believe that they too will share these things with their children.

Grandma didn't have a magic formula for living. She simply had a way of turning hardship into something worthwhile. ✮

Building a Nation

Chapter Two

⋆ ⋆ ⋆ ⋆ ⋆

At the beginning of the 20th century we were still just on the frontiers of the Industrial Revolution. Electricity, automobiles, air travel and many other modern marvels were in their infancy, but still just a pipe dream to most Americans.

Those who built a nation into a world superpower took that pipe dream and made it a reality. Despite two world wars and a debilitating Great Depression, from factory and farm, from inspiration to perspiration, they pieced together the underpinnings of a great country.

It was that crucible of adversity that made steelworkers and road builders, construction engineers and small-time inventors realize they were a small part of something much larger. Instead of allowing that adversity to buckle them, these men and women climbed from the cauldron of desperation and forged a better way of life.

This chapter is dedicated to those who built the roads and bridges, those who harnessed the unrelenting power of the river and the wind, those who filled factories and oil fields with strength and hope.

Though their names may not be listed in the annals of history, these men and women were the soldiers on the front lines of progress. Their names may be forgotten, but they, too, had a strong hand in building a nation.

—*Ken Tate*

Left: Boatyards provided those great vessels that plied the rivers, waterways and seas, moving the economic giant of the world. In this mural, Grand Propeller, *artist Robert Dafford captured the blinding flash of the welder's work. The mural is part of a major collection painted by Dafford's team of artists on the flood wall along the Ohio River at Paducah, Ky.*

Pick & Shovel Soldiers

By Donald F. Kraack

We once referred to it as "flop, slop and a dollar a day." The food was Army fare, simple but nutritious. Most of the time it was good, although sometimes it was bad—and usually, it was monotonous. Two of the most popular and frequent "entrees" were the notorious chipped beef on toast and (in my opinion) the unpalatable hominy grits.

Bedding consisted of an Army blanket to lie on, another one and a "comforter," or small quilt, for cover, a light canvas tick filled with straw, and an Army cot for the tent camps. Our winter barracks each contained 50 sets of double-tiered, hard, pine, slat-bottomed, 3-feet-wide bunks. We supplied our own pillow.

The clothing issue was a combination of Army and Navy World War I surplus. We took what was given us, with no complaints. I was issued denim fatigue trousers that wrapped around me twice. After deliberately wearing them with a rope belt for two weeks, I was considered a potential disgrace to our outfit and was ordered to the quartermaster for a decent fit. Thereafter, my size was never debated.

Without pinning the blame on any one individual or party, the nation was, to put it mildly, in one heck of a mess.

The work was hard for those who could and would take it. Most of us did, with few exceptions, depending on which foreman we were placed with.

Despite hardships, and what many thought to be a spartan way of living, the Civilian Conservation Corps—the "three C's," as it was commonly called—was a godsend and a lifesaver to thousands of men and boys. It was especially a blessing to the impoverished down-and-outers who could almost literally wipe their faces with the slack of their bellies, being only a few short turns from the long soup lines.

In the summer of 1933, our recently elected president, Franklin Delano Roosevelt, had almost immediately begun tightening reins to bring misery and runaway privation under control.

For at least four years since the stock market crash of 1929, despondent, desperate citizens who had been ruined financially had been committing suicide by almost every conceivable means. Without pinning the blame on any one individual or party, the nation was, to put it mildly, in one heck of a mess. Something had to be done, and fast, so Roosevelt implemented several stopgap measures to put the wobbly country back on firm legs. The CCC was one of these programs, and while it didn't eliminate the soup and breadlines immediately, it shortened them considerably.

That summer I turned 20 years of age. I had been farming for my grandparents with whom I lived, but after Grandfather passed away in 1932, Grandmother leased out all of the farmland.

Although we were not impoverished or destitute, I found myself "high and dry," jobwise.

Mainly through the efforts of A.B. Andrus, a family friend and neighbor who was on the selection board, I was one of those chosen from St. George, Utah, to go to camp. The date was set when the selectees would depart for Pine Valley, Utah, one of the many camps that had been activated about a month earlier.

The day before our scheduled departure, I was roaming the town's business district with nothing to do. It was hot, sultry and almost unbearable. I noticed an Army truck backed to the curb at the old Mathis Market, loading supplies for the camp commissary. Impetuosity overwhelmed me. *Why not go to camp today? Now! Why take this heat another day?* I would be leaving with the quota tomorrow anyway. It was to be a new adventure and I was anxious to get going.

I broached my desire to the two CCC boys loading the truck, explaining that I was to leave for camp tomorrow, but I sure wanted to ride back with them today. I had nothing else to do, and besides, it was cool some 30-odd miles into the mountains.

I grabbed a bleached flour sack, throwing into it personal items such as soap, towels and toothbrush. After a hasty goodbye to Grandmother, I dashed back to the truck.

They were most reluctant to take me at first, but after much persuasion, they finally agreed. They said they were leaving as soon as the truck was loaded, so I ran the couple of blocks home, grabbed a bleached flour sack, throwing into it personal items such as soap, towels and toothbrush. After a hasty goodbye to Grandmother, I dashed back to the truck.

About sunset we arrived at the Pine Valley camp, and I noticed that they were still in the process of constructing lumber buildings. I had created somewhat of a problem by arriving a day ahead of time; they were just not prepared for me. They thought it was unorthodox and strange that I wanted to come to camp a day before schedule. However, I was shown to the mess hall for my evening meal; the others had already eaten earlier.

I was later thrown a canvas tick and was directed to "fill 'er up" at a straw pile behind the tents. I was tossed an Army blanket, and was

Civilian Conservation Corps workers dig fence postholes on a project in the 1930s. Photo courtesy of Library of Congress, Prints & Photographs Division, FSA-OWI Collection LC-USF34-044210-D DLC.

Workers in the "Three Cs" logged thousands of acres of land in preparation for CCC projects across the country. Photo courtesy of Library of Congress, Prints & Photographs Division, FSA-OWI Collection LC-USF34-044210-D DLC.

Later that afternoon, the group from St. George arrived. We were given a short briefing: We would be subject to military control while at camp, and to forestry supervision while on the job.

Our captain and C.O. was regular Army on special duty from a Texas cavalry unit. He was a fine-looking soldier, fair but a disciplinarian, somewhat younger than middle-aged and straight as a plumb line right from his strap-under-chin campaign hat to his spurred boots—the type of man you could look on with deep pride.

Our master sergeant was an old campaigner from the Spanish-American war, Mexican border trouble and World War I, and he looked it. He was soon due for retirement and probably none too soon. Chain-smoking and a hacking cough had given him a caved-in chest with a consumptive look. We young bucks enjoyed visiting his tent at night after chow, just to hear him spin his never-ending tales of conquests. He was a dead ringer for the old English actor George Arliss, even in his manner of speech.

Our mess sergeant was also regular Army, while our doctor, or doctors (who frequently came and went, one at a time), were Army and Navy Reserves. Each doctor had responsibility for three or more camps, with a first-aid man always on duty in each camp, especially during the doctors' absence.

We were all assigned to specific work crews for tasks such as road building, constructing recreation areas in the mountains, fencing, blasting, bridge building, flood control and anything else that needed to be done, including conservation work, as our title implied.

Division was six men to a tent, integrating individuals from towns throughout Utah and the boys from Virginia.

directed to a tent where I could spend the night on the board floor. I would be issued the rest of my bedding, clothes and gear when the other enrollees arrived on the morrow. I spent a miserable night. For several weeks, not being used to wool blankets, it seemed they literally tore holes in my skin.

Next morning, after an early breakfast, I was instructed to help dig excavations for more permanent buildings I was placed with some boys from Virginia.

A fellow who was shoveling out dirt down in a trench called up to a boy for a drink of water from his belt canteen. A seemingly hard-boiled young lad, a Virginian of Italian ancestry, spoke up and said, "Give him a drink—heck! Kick him in the face!"

This kind of talk was somewhat unusual to a farm boy. I looked at him and thought, *What kind of a character is he?* But when I later got acquainted with the kid, we became fast friends. I discovered this was just his way of talking and his method of impressing newcomers to camp. Nothing malicious or belligerent was intended. This was my introduction to Camp F-24, CCC Company No. 1335, Pine Valley, and eventually Leeds, Utah.

As in most large concentrations of men from small towns and cities, (our complement was 200-plus) we had every type imaginable—college graduates, skilled laborers, artists, musicians, family men, cultured high-class men who had once been well-to-do. We also had the degenerates and dregs of the gutters, ex-convicts and some of the lowest types possible in our society, all thrown in together and trying to stay alive on $30 per month, $25 of which was sent home, with the remaining $5 allowed to the enrollee. Would citizens settle for anything similar now? I don't think so.

I had been placed with a crew that built recreation sites, installed stoves and camping facilities, etc. Our foreman, Tom Muir, was from northern Utah; he was a working fool, but he was good to his men. Tom claimed that Jack Dempsey, the former boxing champ, had been a personal friend when he had been at the pinnacle of his career. During lunch breaks each day, Tom always entertained the crew with a new vignette about Dempsey, which emphasized the champ's generosity.

Each member of the camp took his turn at night guard duty, but instead of being issued a weapon, we were provided with an ax. In case of a tent fire from the Sibley-type stoves, the guy ropes were to be cut, immediately dropping the tent and thereby preventing flames from spreading.

All living quarters, with the exception of headquarters personnel, were tents. The recreation and mess halls, quartermasters, laundry and shower houses were lumber barracks-type buildings. The latrine building was ample and durable.

Those boys who had never done pick-and-shovel work soon adapted themselves, especially when told, "Fill up the 'heel' of the shovel; the 'toe' will take care of itself."

Most of us worked hard and ate hearty. The stiff regimen, wholesome food, mountain air

All living quarters, with the exception of headquarters personnel, were tents. The recreation and mess halls, quartermasters, laundry and shower houses were lumber barracks-type buildings.

and regular hours kept us in fine fettle. We all had at least one thing in common: hard times, which proved to be a great leveler. Our camp had a good reputation in St. George where most of us spent our weekends on passes. We were frequently entertained in camp by some of the more talented townspeople.

Some of the other camps in our area didn't fare so well. They had more than their share of hell-raisers, and this often presented a genuine problem for the town's natives.

I had been about four or five weeks on forest work when one evening, as I was crossing the company street to wash for chow, Storey, a Virginian and our first-aid man, stopped me. He said, "Don, we Virginians are being transferred back home in a couple of weeks, and I would like you to take over my job when we go."

"Thanks," I said, "but I don't know anything about first aid, and I'm not too sure I could handle it even if I did." But Storey assured me I could learn, and said that he would arrange with headquarters to have me stay in camp for the next two weeks to train and study.

I accepted reluctantly. If needed, I would be on call 24 hours a day while in camp, short of occasional passes, and then it would be my responsibility to find someone to replace me temporarily. The job had plenty of drawbacks, but I was to receive $15 a month extra—$45 total—and that looked big to me. (As it turned out, I never did receive my extra $15; it disappeared somewhere between the government disburser and our payroll officer. I was just naive enough to believe that if I protested, I would risk my job in the Corps, so I foolishly said nothing.)

The new job, with few exceptions, was clean work, but I never knew so many men could have headaches, get constipated, involve themselves in knife fights, various kinds of poisonings, cuts and bruises, and just be plain "gold bricks." I was continually dispensing CC (constant constipation) pills by the handfuls; it seemed the mountain drinking water was good, but hard. Iodine was our only germicide, and I frequently mixed a gallon at a time from iodine crystals and alcohol. (There were plenty of yells in every bottle.)

I retained the position throughout the rest of the summer and into the fall. With the coming of colder weather, they began to push completion of our winter barracks at Leeds, Utah, and many of the men were sent down to get work rolling at our new campsite.

In an effort to beat city rents, many a husband brought his wife and children to the mild climate of Leeds, placing them in tents outside the government compound. Barbering, poker playing, a foremanship, or anything else for that extra bit of income was eagerly sought to keep the family intact and fed.

In an effort to beat city rents, many a husband brought his wife and children, placing them in tents outside the government compound.

I remained at Pine Valley until the last remnant of men pulled out. When I arrived at Leeds, I found another fellow already in the first-aid position. He seemed to want the job quite badly, and since it was beginning to wear pretty thin for me anyway, I figured I had found my chance to dump it. The boy was welcome to it, although he soon found the work disenchanting.

I signed for another six-month hitch, going back into the mountains on an efficient road-building crew. I got on the gang of Woodruff Cannon, an engineer and contractor, also a St. George native I had known. His whole crew got along fine. In those days we thought more of pride in our work than the money we earned.

Most of the work was manual, using pick and shovel, with a few teams and scrapers, or Fresnos. We had but one air compressor for pneumatic drilling and one small bulldozer. For awhile a big, husky German, only five years from the old country, was paired with me. We were a drilling team. I turned the drill, and he swung the sledge. Everytime he came down on the drill, apprehension almost got the better of me. I kept thinking, *there go my hands this time*, but he never missed, and we blasted roads out of solid rock.

Cannon saw to it that his crew received the choicest food possible. He figured that with the brand of work his men were putting out, we deserved the best. If the food brought from camp was not hot or worthy, he was the first to sling it from his mess kit.

After three months from the second sign-up, our camp was discontinued and the equipment and personnel were moved to Idaho. This was in the spring of 1934. Those who wanted to go could do so, or we could enter another local camp. I elected to do neither, but took a chance on the uncertain job market.

According to *The Statistical History of the United States from Colonial Times to the Present*, manpower in the Civilian Conservation Corps reached its zenith in 1935 at 459,000 members, up from 290,000 in 1933 when it began.

World War II clouds began to gather soon after this, and a modicum of employment started to show in defense preparations around the country. From then on, the CCC steadily declined to 126,000 men. It was finally phased out altogether in 1942.

The peak year of earnings was 1935, when CCC workers earned $332,851,000, probably an infinitesimal figure by today's standards. But it represented a good-sized payroll back in Depression times.

But more than giving each corpsman the chance to make a little money, working in the CCC helped preserve his independence and dignity. It taught him skills and gave him the know-how to go on to bigger and better endeavors. Above all, it taught him to have faith and confidence in a crippled nation that had the guts to pull itself up by its bootstraps from the mire of despondency. ☆

My CCC Days

By Thomas Tarantino

The Civilian Conservation Corps was created in 1933, and I know it holds nostalgic memories for many fine men.

So many young men were unemployed and destitute during the Depression. The idea was born for a peaceful army, working to preserve and develop America's natural resources. This was when I joined the CCC.

The first groups, like ours, really roughed it. We had no nice barracks or other comforts. Our group was one of the first to leave Fort Sheridan for Camp Brinks Co. 640, near Washburn, Wis. Most of us were from Chicago and Milwaukee. All of us were part of the Great Depression, and felt that perhaps life in the CCC camp would help.

The train ride to Camp Brinks was really rough, especially since many of us had colds from the bad weather at Fort Sheridan. We were really tired by the time the train pulled into Washburn. And when we arrived, we were told that we still had 18 miles to walk to reach Camp Brinks.

After marching six miles, we were allowed to stop and rest. We were served cold bologna sandwiches—plain, with no butter or mustard on stale bread—and black coffee.

Many of us wondered how we were going to march the remaining 12 miles. Luckily, some of the boys got wind that they had stake trucks in camp. We all went on strike and refused to walk any farther, and one of the boys told the commanding officer to get the truck there.

We were tired and sleepy, but we were in for another shock—there was no place for us to sleep. We were told that if we intended to sleep inside that night, we had better start pitching our tents!

After two hours, the trucks finally arrived, and we rode the final 12 miles to Camp Brinks. We were tired and sleepy, but we were in for another shock—there was no place for us to sleep. We were told that if we intended to sleep inside that night, we had better start pitching our tents!

The next surprise was that we had no bathroom facilities! The only thing we could do was go off into the woods. I was one of the boys assigned to the detail to build outhouses. We had instructions to build 12; as a joke, we built 13—all in a row. Many boys went home with some good pictures of the group using those "deluxe" bathrooms!

My job was to dynamite old stumps and build a fire lane. We also planted many pine trees—sometimes 1,000–1,100 trees a day. Many years later, when I visited Washburn, it was something to see those trees standing so tall.

For excitement we used to go into town when they held dances at the town hall. One of the boys would buy a ticket for the dance, and they would pin a ribbon to his lapel that allowed him to go in and out of the dance hall freely.

Then one of the boys would go purchase enough matching ribbon for all our jackets so that we could all get in free. Most of us had so little cash. The CCC sent $25 to our parents each month, and we were left with only $5 a month.

I often wonder what has become of all those boys from the CCC. I left camp after six months. I declined to re-enlist; I don't like roughing it, and still hate the idea of camping. ☆

That Old Covered Bridge

By Halsey McCleod

Old covered bridges fascinate me—partly because there are so few left, but mainly because of my boyhood association with them.

About a mile west of our small hill farm, one of these spanned Raccoon Creek, a good-sized stream that, in the drier Southwest where I live today, probably would have been called a river. We swam in it and fished its waters with hickory poles. There were several such bridges over the old Raccoon as it meandered through the hills to the Ohio River.

The cover, or roof, protected the wooden bridge from rapid decay, and provided shade for a farmer's team if he felt they needed a brief rest out of reach of the hot summer sun. Sometimes the sudden approach of a thundershower would nudge them forward to reach the shelter before the downpour began.

Not far from the entrance to our bridge was an old deserted house, reputed to be haunted. I didn't believe in ghosts, although I was afraid of them. The sighing of the breeze among the bridge's rafters, and the creaking and snapping

of wooden joints as they contracted and expanded in response to changes in temperature and humidity were spooky sounds to begin with—and they seemed even more so in the dark, silent night.

Automobiles were virtually unknown to us back then, and I had no horse and buggy. So, when I attended such social functions as our rural area afforded—spelling bees, box lunch socials, etc.—I traveled, to use a colloquial expression, by shank's mare. In other words, I walked.

My return home often took me across the covered bridge after dark. Before entering, I would grasp a rock in each hand. Then I would rapidly march straight ahead, looking neither right nor left, and whistle as loudly as I could to drown out any eerie sounds. If a ghost had wanted to sneak up behind me and clout me over the head, I never would have been the wiser.

Goodbye, old covered bridge. It was nice to know you. ☆

☆☆☆☆☆☆☆☆☆☆☆☆☆☆☆

A Road Construction Camp of Years Ago

By Eva Bolland

A road construction camp was my summer home during my childhood in the 1920s and early 1930s. The camp was a collection of mobile sheds where the men and mules who built the roads were housed and fed.

Most people were shocked to find my mother in the cook car. "Bull cooks" were expected. In the early years, we knew of no other women or children in road camps. Later, female cooks became common, and wives and children began to live with their men at the camps in separate houses-on-wheels, the fore-runners of today's mobile homes.

The men toiled 60-hour weeks in the heat and dust. Sometimes cursed by their bosses, still, they were glad to have jobs. Slopers were paid 75 cents, teamsters $1.25, and machine operators $3 per day, plus "keep." They were often too exhausted to play horseshoes after work. They flopped onto the ground, fighting mosquitoes until the bunk cars cooled off enough to sleep in them.

The breakfast gong awakened me at 6 a.m. I heard the men enter the nearby cook car. My mother scolded someone who hadn't cleaned his boots. I opened my eyes briefly, viewing my tiny shed-bedroom in half of the family bunk car. There was nothing to see but my clothing hanging on the wall nails above my feet. My father, who was the owner and boss of the road construction company, and my mother, who was the cook, had their bed beyond the partition. Some clothing was kept under the beds, where the company files were also stored.

The family bunk car was mounted on two wheels. In camp, the wheels were dug down and blocks were placed under corners. On treeless campsites, guy wires were fastened to the upper corners and were staked to the ground.

I was awakened again when the catskinners cranked their Caterpillar tractors to life. I heard the teamsters (muleskinners) yelling abusively as they hitched their teams to dump wagons. Closer by was the clatter of dishwashing. My fat tummy was demanding bread and syrup so I pulled on my dress and dipped water from a cream can to wash my hands in one of the basins on a bench outside the cook car.

As I shooed the flies and entered, I saw Mama rolling pie crusts on the zinc-topped worktable, under which were bins of flour and sugar. A pot roast bubbled in the big roaster over two burners of the gas range.

We had no cupboards, so I put away the breakfast dishes by setting the table for dinner. At each of the 16 places, I placed a fork and knife and covered them with an overturned plate.

The 20- by 8-foot cook car had a cabinet by the door. Dried and canned supplies filled shelves and every corner. After opening a gallon can of loganberries for Mama's pies, I hastily finished my stewed prunes, grabbed a handful of cheap cookies and disappeared outdoors.

A girl about my size and her mother were passing on the road. Hoping to find a playmate, I called out a greeting. "Don't talk to that gypsy girl!" warned the mother.

The barn boss was cleaning the barn—a long building on four wheels, with mangers for 10 horses on each side. The roof was supported by six hinged poles, and when the barn was moved, the roof and poles folded against the mangers. The barn had no sides or ends except during winter shutdown, when a panel with a small window was set in place behind each team.

In the days before the routine use of heavy equipment, sheer strength in numbers provided the manpower to build roads across the nation. Here a road construction crew in 1920 prepares a road bed in Colorado with the help of a single bulldozer and a pair of one-ton trucks. Photo courtesy Denver Public Library, Western History Collection Rh-4501.

An acetylene-welding torch threw sparks in the machine repair shop. This shop traveled on four wheels, but the front two were removed in camp. The workbench covered the rear wheels. The shop was large enough for tractors to be repaired inside. Hinged panels swung down to form the lower part of the walls, but now they were up and the big doors were open for ventilation.

I wandered to the two bunk cars, which provided crude sleeping quarters for the workmen. Bedsprings and mattresses (or straw ticks) were placed on wooden frames to form double/double-decker bunks that held four men each. I climbed on these, but the sweaty smell soon drove me outside.

Machine noises and clouds of dust told me the road was being built a short distance from camp. I decided to watch.

A Cat (track-type tractor) pulled a mucker (elevating grader) back and forth along the "cut," plowing up and loading dirt onto dump wagons. A teamster stood, whip ready, watching behind as dirt with rocks was spilled off the mucker belt into his wagon. He had to keep his wagon—but not himself—under the moving belt. Sometimes he had to whip his team frantically. Then he could sit as his team pulled the load to the "dump" where fill was needed. The dump boss stood there, signaling each teamster where to drive and when to dump, by pulling the lever that opened the wagon's hinged bottom.

Some distance away, my father was leveling off the previous cut-and-fill; that is, he was finishing that stretch of road. The blade (blading grader or maintainer) was not self-propelled as such machines are today, but was pulled by a Cat. Daddy moved the big wheels that controlled the blade and also kept signaling to the catskinner exactly where to drive. Catskinners rode sideways in their seats, watching behind more than ahead.

When I saw Shorty driving to the cook car with cream cans of fresh water, I knew I had to run in order to perform those few dinner chores required of me. One of those chores was crawling under one end of the cook car to dig butter from a buried crock, as we had no refrigeration.

The intense heat inside the cook car didn't stop me from inhaling appreciatively the smell of roast meat and fresh pies. It was fun to hammer the dinner gong, a mucker disk fastened near the cook car door. The men trooped in, one of them daring to enter without a shirt. Mama said he looked like meat and got her enormous knife. He went after a shirt.

Road construction camps are only a memory today—along with Mama's scolding, the flies buzzing, and the great food! ☆

Road Trash

By Freda Ackerman

There was a time when "road trash" referred not to litter along highways; rather, it was what some people called the good, hardworking men and their families who had built the roads in the first place. They moved back and forth across this land, and they had to prove themselves everywhere they went.

My family was what some folks called "road trash." By the time the natives decided we might be all right, it was time to move on. I'm sure we all had our faults the same as anyone else, but somehow they seemed worse to a stranger.

It wasn't all bad, though. Dad started as a blade man on a horse-drawn machine; he made good money, always drawing the going wage. But we never accumulated anything because we moved so often, and we had to throw away or give away most of it each time.

Once a local woman kept coming by and asking Mom what she was going to do with a Jenny Lind bed she had. She kept saying, "I guess you will just have to throw that away," never offering to buy it for even a modest price.

Finally Mom got mad, saying, "I expect I'll just take the ax and chop it up for kindling!" But she didn't. We gave the bed to the pastor's wife.

There were two gangs—the bridge gang and the dirt gang. The bridge gang went first and built the culverts and bridges, and cleared the way for the dirt gang. The bridge gang used a lot of nails, so they had nail kegs to use for chairs and all sorts of furniture. The dirt gang didn't have kegs, but had wonderful dynamite boxes. Were they ever grand! We could make chairs, desks, dressing tables, hens' nests and lots more. It was a standing joke that you could tell the bridge gang by the round rings on their behinds, while the dirt gang's were rectangular.

We lived in everything from a tent to a two-story house, depending on how close we were to the job or how many kids we had in the family. We started out pretty well, getting fairly nice places. But by the time all five of us had appeared, it wasn't so easy. Then it was, "Lord, anything will do, as long as we have a roof over our heads."

When we moved to Chanute, Kan., Dad went on ahead and found us a place. He outdid himself—a pretty house, even a bathroom, and in a good part of town. We didn't see how we came to be so lucky. It turned out that a young girl had been electrocuted in the bathtub by faulty wiring and everyone thought the house was haunted. We thanked the supposed ghost and lived in splendor for a few weeks.

It was while we lived there that I found out there was no Santa Claus. What the heck? I thought. You can't have everything. We had a bathroom; who needed St. Nick?

Sometimes we lived so close to a job that when they yelled, "Fire in the hole!" we crawled under the bed in case some of the rocks came through the roof. It was a little frightening, as well as exciting. I can still smell the smoke hanging in the air, like sniffing down the barrel of a newly fired gun, multiplied many times over.

"Road trash"—that was what we were called. But the next time you drive down one of our great highways, tip your hat to those wonderful, big-hearted, hardworking men who built them, and to their families who followed them on jobs across this great country. ✪

It was a standing joke that you could tell the bridge gang by the round rings on their behinds, while the dirt gang's were rectangular.

Kinzua Bridge: An Engineering Wonder

By Francis X. Sculley

As if the city were being evacuated in the face of an invading foreign army, hundreds jammed, wiggled, squirmed and shoved their way into each of the 14 special railway cars lining the Buffalo railway platform. Within a few moments, another 14 cars from Rochester joined the bedlam, all crowded to the doors with squealing, shouting passengers. As the 28 fully loaded cars left the station, a few latecomers, their picnic hampers almost as jammed as the train cars, were helped up the iron steps by the conductor. No one was to be left behind on this wonderful Sabbath morning.

To the south, in Pittsburgh, the same process was repeated, and all the way along the line to the north, extra coaches were added to the train as it wended its way through the mountains toward the "eighth wonder of the world."

On that Sunday morning, June 18, 1883, 60 cars finally disgorged thousands of shirtsleeved Americans at both ends of the world's longest railroad bridge—"the engineering feat of the ages," as it had been described in newspapers and magazines.

That afternoon, writers from Pennsylvania's great city newspapers, viewing the picnickers below the great span, described it as looking like a vast military encampment.

As hundreds tiptoed across the bridge, 301 feet above the gorge below, it teetered in the breeze, sending scores scurrying to the ends in panic. Here and there, some of the more daring, perhaps inspired by the contents of their hampers, tried to climb the great structure, only to be chased off by the bridge master, Charley Stauffer. Later in the afternoon, the inspector thrilled the thousands when he climbed one of the great towers with his little son on his back.

For three decades, summer excursions from America's greatest cities to the Kinzua Viaduct continued. It was estimated that by the start of World War I, more than a million had made the trip to the mecca of vacationers.

Kinzua Bridge was built in 1882 in just 105 working days by Anthony Bonzano of the Phoenixville Bridge Co. The great bridge builder had told General Thomas Kane, creator of the famed Bucktail Regiment, "We'll build you a bridge a thousand feet high, if you'll provide the money."

Forty men started the project on the 10th day of May. Using only a gin pole, the first tower was erected in less than a week. A wooden crane built at the top of the first tower was used to place the ironwork of the second tower, and so on. There were 20 towers in all. Stone from the hillsides above provided the footings for the great viaduct. Imbedded as much as 35 feet below the surface, and bonded, the footings were joined to the bridge by half-inch bolts, 6–10 feet in length.

The legs of the supporting towers were flanged, wrought-iron columns, 9¾ inches in diameter, spliced at every panel. Additional supporting columns ascended to the fifth story midway between the legs of the tallest towers.

The completed bridge swayed like a hammock. Trains were restricted to 5 miles an hour when crossing, else every train would have been swept from the tracks. Often, open gondolas had their cargo blown out, and there have been recorded incidents of boxcars being unroofed by the awesome winds that whip

down the gorge. Workmen have often described how difficult it was for the trackwalker to keep his footing atop the teetering bridge.

To millions of Americans, the bridge was the most thrilling sight in the world. In the fall, when the foliage of Pennsylvania's northern woodlands was aflame, the track paths were lined with picnicking families as they headed for the hillsides to have dinner and view the bridge. Holidays always brought special attraction to Kinzua, either in the form of the awesome climb by Charley Stauffer, or an attempt to walk the 3-inch wooden railing at the top. Once a man made it over the bridge with a horse and wagon, with the shaking equine gently tiptoeing from tie to tie, with nothing but air below.

By 1900, the $167,000 the bridge cost to build had been many times recovered from excursionists alone, and no one could estimate how many millions of tons of freight had passed over the bridge that always swayed like a hula dancer.

But eventually, heavier rolling stock came into general use. So, in 1900, the bridge was torn down and rebuilt by Octave Chanute, who would one day have an air base named in his honor. The highest tower and its adjoining spans were demolished in one day, an awesome feat. Progress moved at the rate of 50 feet per month during the reconstruction. It took but seven and one-half days to rebuild the original tower and the crew of 100 rebuilt the bridge in less than four months, completing it during a raging forest fire that destroyed two villages below.

While excursions to the bridge were suspended during World War I, thousands of Americans from every state continued to visit the great structure three miles south of the village on Mount Jewett. On Aug. 12, 1963, Gov. William Scranton established the Kinzua Viaduct as a state park, and on July 5, 1975, the swaying structure was dedicated as thousands stood atop the beloved bridge, just as many of them had done since childhood.

Many men and women have scaled the bridge, although it is not encouraged, as trouble always occurs when the top of the tower is reached, to get above the jutting ironwork.

Larry Peace, a former professional football player, made it hand over hand from one end to the other, a distance of 2,053 feet, and 301 feet above the rocks. While the athlete was making this crossing, a freight train puffed overhead, inching its way across the swaying structure, as the powerful young man hung precariously by his fingers. In later years, the Bradford, Pa., man always insisted that he had no idea a train was on its way across.

One afternoon, two youngsters walked the three-inch-wide railing atop the length of the bridge. Luckily, there was no wind that day, or the walker on the east side would have been swept into the gorge.

When General U.S. Grant spoke from Kinzua Bridge in November 1883, 4,000 citizens listened to the Union's all-conquering soldier talk about the wonders of progress. Later, both presidents McKinley and Roosevelt were to visit the structure.

Kinzua Bridge is one of the highest and longest railroad bridges in North America. No railroad crossing can lay claim to exceeding it in both height and length.

Featured in more than 100 magazines and newspapers since the time of *Harper's Weekly* and *Century*, the ancient bridge, built in less time than many homes, still stands as one of the most nostalgic spots in the East. And many who visit the bridge once are drawn back to it again. ☆

The black-and-white photographs on the facing page and at top were all taken around the turn of the 20th century at the Kinzua Bridge, one of the longest railroad bridges in North America. The color photographs above were taken nearly a century later. All photos © courtesy Route-6.com and the Mt. Jewett (Pa.) Chamber of Commerce.

They Were "Boulder" by a Dam Site

By Harry Squires

On June 5 and 6, 1983, more than 400 men who had helped build Boulder Dam (now called Hoover Dam) gathered in Boulder City, Nev., to celebrate the 50th anniversary of the pouring of the first bucket of concrete for the dam.

What manner of men built this colossus? What brought them from every corner of the nation to a godforsaken, roadless desert wasteland to hold back a rampaging river? Were they human, or as savage as the river they tried to restrain?

Men flocked by the thousands to the heat-scorched Nevada site in search of work. In those days, with the nation in the midst of an economic depression, people fought for any kind of job. At one time the town site, today the community of Boulder City, housed more than 7,000 workers.

The first police officer hired to keep order was Bill Getts, who had been a Texas Ranger for 11 years. Getts served for 30 years as a Hoover Dam lawman and was living in retirement in his home in Boulder City when I talked to him.

Top: A magnificent view of Hoover Dam. Above: Tons of earth had to be moved in preparation for the building of the dam. Right: Early work begins on the narrow canyon carved by the Colorado River that became the site of Hoover Dam. All photos courtesy U.S. Department of the Interior, Bureau of Reclamation, Lower Colorado Region, Hoover Dam.

"Our police force, at the height of construction, consisted of only nine men," Getts told me. "The men who worked on the dam were the roughest, toughest, most ornery bunch of men ever placed on God's earth. Sunday supplement editors used to refer to us as the toughest police in the nation," he added with a smile.

The manager of the campsite was a small, slight man who ruled the workers with an iron hand. His name was Sims Ely, but among themselves, the men called him "the little tin god." Ely was a stern practitioner and expounder of the moral code. He had little patience for bootleggers, drunks or thieves.

When early work in the canyon began (above), who would have guessed that the engineers and builders (bottom) of Hoover Dam would be able to successfully plug the canyon and tame the waters of the mighty Colorado (below)?

"If a Ranger brought a man to Ely's office for an infraction involving one of these crimes," Getts said, "Ely would go through a ritual whose meaning was clear to the Ranger. The camp manager would open the center drawer of his desk and reach for the man's personnel file. As Ely studied the man's record, the Ranger who arrested the man would watch Ely's movements closely. If the manager moved his eyeglasses to the tip of his long, thin nose and nonchalantly started to comb his thinning hair, the Ranger knew that the man was to be immediately driven to the main gate and told firmly that he was *persona non grata* forever at the campsite."

For the first time in the history of the river, men descended into the riverbed and laid the foundations for the dam. Seven million tons of concrete had to be laid down, enough concrete to build a 16-foot-wide road across the United States.

Around the clock, 24 hours a day, for more than two years, the pouring of the concrete continued. Under the hot desert sun by day and under powerful floodlights by night, the pouring never let up.

"The dam builders worked in an abbreviated attire, consisting of diggers—Levis of red canvas cloth—and hard hats," Getts recalled. "When they came off shift with the muck and the sweat on their faces and in their hair, they shed their diggers and walked stark naked from the barracks to the community shower. This was a

A huge conduit (right and above) became a water bypass around the Hoover Dam construction site. The bypass allowed the pouring of millions of cubic feet of concrete to complete the construction of the dam (pictured nearing completion below).

series of barrels sus-pended above what is now the railroad depot. One man got underneath the barrel while another man upended the barrel with a pull-chain."

When the construction man was not working, he spent his time drinking and fighting. Just beyond the main gate to the construction site was Railroad Pass, a combination saloon and restaurant. It was each man for himself at Railroad Pass, and heaven help the man with a weak stomach. Practically every night, men fought with fists, knives, broken beer bottles and odd pieces of saloon furniture.

"Close to Railroad Pass," reminisced Getts, "were several tent towns with colorful names. For example, I recall there was Texas Acres and, believe me, the men who lived there were like buckets of blood. These tent towns had fights among themselves, and when one tent town waged 'war' on a neighboring one, it kept us marshals hopping to restore order."

At last, the concrete pouring was done, the cables were cut down, and the derricks, trucks and electric shovels were moved. The bypasses were blocked up, and the rushing waters of the Colorado River flowed again after more than two years of confinement.

Then came the moment that turns engineers' hair white. Would the dam hold? Had the computations, graphs, charts and years of backbreaking work been in vain?

Thousands lined the canyon walls as the pent-up fury of the river hit the dam. The water surged forward and pounded the dam relentlessly.

"She's holding! She's holding!" thousands shouted, and their joy echoed across the canyon.

On Sept. 30, 1935, President Franklin D. Roosevelt dedicated the dam while more than 10,000 persons watched and listened. To the workers, the chief executive said, "Well done!"

Later, on Feb. 29, 1936, Frank T. Crowe, general superintendent for the six construction companies that built the dam, shook hands with Ralph Lowry, Reclamation Service engineer, and merely said, "Take it; it's yours now." ☆

☆☆☆☆☆☆

The Men Who Died

Editor's Note: The following information comes from the Bureau of Reclamation, the federal department now in charge of Hoover Dam.—KT

How many people died building Hoover Dam? How many of those are buried in the concrete? These questions are among those most asked by people who come to Hoover Dam and take the tour of the facility.

The second question is the easiest to answer. There are no bodies buried in the concrete.

The dam was built in interlocking blocks, built on top of each other as they went. Each block was five feet in depth. The smallest blocks were about 25 by 25 feet, and the largest blocks were about 25 by 60 feet. Concrete was delivered to the blocks in buckets, eight cubic yards at a time. After each bucket was delivered, five or six men would tromp around on the inside of the block, packing down the concrete and making sure there were no air holes. These men were called "puddlers."

Each time a bucket was emptied into the largest blocks the level of the concrete increased by two to three inches. How can you lose a body in two to three inches of concrete? Of course, the smaller blocks did fill up faster. Each time a bucket was emptied into the smaller blocks the level was raised about six inches. Even with six inches the puddlers

would have seen them. There are no bodies buried in Hoover Dam. In fact, we call that a dam rumor.

The first question is more difficult to answer. There are various numbers that can be used depending on who you include as having died on the project. One popular number is 112, but it requires some stretching to make it fit. With this number you get the story of the first and last men to die on the project. It goes something like this.

On Dec. 20, 1922, J.G. Tierney, a Bureau of Reclamation employee engaged in a geological survey from a barge in the Colorado River fell in the river and drowned.

Thirteen years to the day, on Dec. 20, 1935, Patrick W. Tierney, a Bureau or Reclamation employee and son of J.G. Tierney, fell from one of the intake towers.

This version has a couple of problems. First, the dam was built from 1931 to 1935, so J.G. Tierney was not really involved in the "construction" of the dam. He was doing a geological survey to decide where the dam would be built, but he was not the first person doing the survey to die.

On May 15, 1922, Harold Connelly, also fell off of a barge and drowned. So, why isn't he considered the first person to die on the project? Well, for one thing it would not make as good a story as the Tierney family. To get around this people point out that Connelly died while surveying a canyon upstream from the present site of the dam, while both Tierneys died in the canyon where the dam was eventually built. ☆

Seboomook Venture

By Bill Thomas

Bunkhouse at Seboomook Dam.

Editor's Note: Not all jobs building dams around the country were like that on the Colorado River. Here is a story of another project in the far north and eastern extreme of the country.—KT

It was in 1935 that four of us young men decided to go to Seboomook, Maine, to get jobs on the dam construction. A local game warden who was going up there gave us a ride. We left on a warm May evening. After passing through Greenville, it was 20 miles to Rockwood, a small community on Moose River, and then 30 miles more through the woods to Seboomook at the head of Moosehead Lake.

Ten miles beyond Rockwood was 10-Mile Field. The Great Northern Paper Co. used to have a hay farm there, about 10 acres. At that time of year, it was just coming up in new grass. Swinging the headlights around the field we could see about 100 deer, feeding on the only grass for miles around.

About midnight we arrived at Seboomook. A man named Irv Hamilton ran the ramshackle hotel there, where hunters, fishermen and woodmen stopped. He also had a little store. About two miles from there was Seboomook Deadwater, on which an old wooden dam was rotting out. We were going to help build a new concrete dam.

We went to the dam site and were hired immediately as laborers at 25 cents per hour.

We worked 60 hours per week and paid $5 a week for our board and room in a long bunkhouse where more than 100 men slept. We ate in another building.

Our first job was to demolish a 10-hole privy that had been built by a lumberjack crew many years earlier. We did that in very short order.

The next morning, we were given shovels and were trucked out to a gravel pit where we shoveled gravel into dump trucks. The trucks at that time only held about two yards of gravel. They hauled it to the dam site and stockpiled it there.

We had six men in our crew. One of them, Rodrigue, got in an argument with the foreman. The next thing we knew he was chasing the foreman through the woods, waving his shovel. The next day, Rodrigue was foreman. We never saw his predecessor again.

On the riverbank near the gravel pit lived an old trapper named Bobcat Bill. He had a dozen pigs that roamed everywhere. It was surprising that a bear did not get some of them. Everyday the pigs came by the gravel pit to a spring brook to play in the water. One of the pigs must have had something wrong with it, for it would sit for hours in the cool water without moving.

If we stayed in camp on Sunday, we would go to Irv Hamilton's store beside the hotel. He had a lot of stock; it was almost a general store. When we asked for beer he would spend at least 10 minutes telling us why he could not sell it on Sunday. Then he

Photographs show Seboomook Dam, partially completed (above), and after completion (bottom).

would say, "How many do you want?"

One Sunday we drove north on a narrow dirt road across the boundary into Canada. The first town was St. Lackery. It was a small town and all the natives spoke French, but by using sign language, we found a hotel where we could get dinner. We were served fried eggs, bacon and potatoes. When we had eaten that, they brought each of us fried chicken, along with vegetables, homemade bread and pickles. Then came wild strawberries, cake and cream. It all cost us 20 cents each.

Back at work on the dam, they dynamited during the evening. Between blasts I fished the pool directly below the foundation site. In those days I caught plenty of trout. I built a wooden box and sank it in an eddy and put live trout in it. Two- and three-pound trout were quite plentiful. I had my 1930 Model-A Ford up there by then, and if we decided to go home for the weekend, I would take a bunch of trout home with me.

My crew transferred to the wharf by the hotel where the steamer Katahdin docked. For several weeks we worked unloading 100-pound bags of cement that had come up the lake from Greenville.

Near the hotel was a pasture where the Great Northern kept about 50 horses. One big black horse would swim out to a little grassy island and stay there all day. He must have been a loner.

Back at the camp we had an one-armed black man for a bull cook. A bull cook is a janitor in a Maine woods camp. His name was Happy and everyone liked him.

Even with only one arm, he could split and lug stovewood and sweep the bunkhouse as well as anyone with two arms.

One day I was promoted to drilling with a jackhammer. I worked it for about two hours before I developed a terrible headache. I was about to throw it into the river when the boss, who must have been watching, came up to me—and that was the end of my drilling. Now I was steelworker. That paid 40 cents an hour—$20 a week take-home pay. That was pretty good in those days. My helper and I lugged a 28-foot bar of 1-inch reinforcing steel into a pier, wired it in place, and then went for another.

By now there was 150 men working. Every week, public cars from Bangor brought in more men. They also took out some who quit, for some men could not stand working 50 miles back in the woods, even when work was scarce.

When we had one pier almost up to its height there was a lot of damage. A new man carried a bucket of bolts to the top edge of the form and made a mistake: He looked down. Fifty feet below, the white water swirled, floating wreckage downstream. He "froze" to the corner of the form. It took six of us to get him back, and we had to hit his fingers with a hammer to make him let go.

Fall was coming and it was too cold to sit outdoors in the evening. The men sat around the bulldog stoves at night and told stories. On the first of November we quit and moved on to other jobs and other ventures. ☆

The children raced upstairs and ran from window to window, calling, "Mama! Daddy! There are lights everywhere! We can see the Jensens, and the Lees—"

EAST VIEW MEMORIES

Jess Hager
'93

The Day the Lights Came On

By Helen D. Mortenson

*I*t was 1938 in the farmland of southern Minnesota. All fall, our section of the county reverberated with the rumble of heavy trucks and bulldozers. Crews of men shouted to one another as they cleared the ditches along the roads for the coming of the REA, the Rural Electrification Administration.

Once the poles were set, it was a thing of beauty to see the sun glint off the new, shiny wire as powerful derricks reeled it off huge wooden spools on the truck and hoisted it up to the lineman to be stretched and counted.

Throughout the county, the air fairly vibrated with anticipation. In the village the usually lethargic hardware and small appliance stores were busy as prospective customers admired newly arrived merchandise. Wherever farmers gathered, REA was the subject that rolled off everyone's tongue.

At the creamery, elevator and bank, men discussed the merits of this milker, that separator or smaller farm tools. In every household, the Montgomery Ward and Sears, Roebuck and Co. catalogs grew dog-eared from farm wives' thumbing, rechecking prices and quality of lighting fixtures, toasters and mixers.

I stopped at my neighbor's one morning and found Marie busy with catalogs, pencil and paper, trying to decide on a light fixture. "I just can't make up my mind," she told me, "and I have to, soon. My brother is using his vacation to help wire the house. But look," she pointed, sighing, "they're all so gorgeous!"

"Oh, I know," I replied. "But I'm looking at washing machines. And I'll be so thankful to be rid of that clumsy old Coleman gas iron."

The door opened as another neighbor came in, laughing. "I saw the car and I knew I'd find you both with the catalogs."

"Coffee's in the pot, Joyce," said our hostess, hardly looking up from her books. "Help yourself."

Joyce flipped the pages of one catalog. "A refrigerator, that's what I want. Imagine being able to set Jell-O in July!"

Once the decision had been made on the most necessary purchases for our farm, we chose a new radio, an elegant one boasting an electric eye to show when a station was accurately tuned in. This powerful model would also bring in foreign stations—a must for my husband, whose hobby was listening to shortwave radio.

And finally, since December was upon us and REA completion had been promised by year's end, we optimistically added several strings of electric Christmas tree lights to our order.

By the third week of December all was ready. Every light switch in our newly wired house, as well as the big yard light, was turned on, waiting for that thrilling moment when some gloved hand threw the lever on the master switch. The anticipation was almost too much to bear.

Two days before Christmas, I was in the kitchen making supper by the light of the Coleman lantern. My husband had just come in from evening chores and the children were playing quietly together in the living room.

Suddenly the radio—turned up as loud as possible, of course—burst on. The Christmas tree lights began to twinkle and blink, and in the dining room, plates and silver set for supper reflected the glow from the fixture above.

For a magical moment in time, everyone was transfixed.

Then the children raced upstairs and ran from window to window, calling, "Mama! Daddy! There are lights everywhere! We can see the Jensens, and the Lees—"

Their excited voices mirrored my own exhilaration as all across the wintry fields, the yard lights of neighboring farms twinkled like stars through the leafless groves—a modern fairyland.

The next morning we were awakened by the melodic chime of our new electric clock. In the early winter light our familiar farmland lay quiet … but we knew that our section of rural America had entered the modern age.

Life "down on the farm" would never be the same again. ✩

My Small Role in the REA

By Esther Payne Davis

If you lived on a farm before 1936 and were already receiving electrical service, you were among the wee minority of one in 10 farmsteads.

Then came 1936, when the Rural Electrification Act brought hope to lantern-carrying farmers everywhere. By providing loan opportunities, President Franklin D. Roosevelt and Congress made it possible for electrical lines to reach rural areas devoid of modern power. Rural electrical cooperatives were formed and farmers dared to dream of actually receiving electric energy for light and work.

My own role with rural electrification began in a small and unsolicited manner. As I heard about electric lines being built in adjoining counties, I became very excited. I realized that this striking change could head in our direction; my old farm home could be flooded with light and power.

Being very anxious for my widowed mother to have electricity, I wanted to become helpful in the program. I approached our local rural electric co-op office and asked if I might take the papers to farmers and urge them to sign for electricity.

The co-op was very obliging; they did not want unserved gaps in the area they were covering, thus stranding farms without power. They were happy to augment my services toward developing comprehensive coverage.

My allies were two of the most progressive farmers in the neighborhood. It was our goal to see that all farmers in our area were contacted and ready to "tie on" when the lines came close to them.

Touring the countryside in my mother's 1936 Chevy in the summer of 1945, I found most of the farmers agreeable. A few were concerned about the possibility of fire with this new electricity and the "high" minimum rate of $2.80 per month.

During those wartime years, farmers also had to qualify for electrical service by using it in ways that would put the new power to work producing more food—such as purchasing a milking machine, a deep-well pump, chicken incubator, etc.

I spent long, arduous but gratifying days on this undertaking. My mother kept my year-old daughter each day I went out, and I sometimes found myself hanging diapers on the clothesline after I returned at dark.

But my time and rationed gasoline were willingly contributed to the cause. We did get electricity much sooner as a result, and all the farmers were ready when the lines came through.

I shall never forget the thrill of that day in April when my old farmhouse shone ablaze with light. It was worth the days I spent bouncing over the hot countryside giving unprofessional, but heartfelt, sales talks on behalf of electricity.

Through the years, I have always felt a secret pride that I might have had a small but helpful hand in more quickly bringing electricity to the part of the country I called home. ✩

This photograph of my husband, daughter and me was taken in November 1945.

Electricity FOR HIM

RURAL ELECTRIFICATION ADMINISTRATION • U.S. DEPT. OF AGRICULTURE

THE REA WAY

AREA COVERAGE. . .ELECTRICITY FOR ALL WHEN NEIGHBORS COOPERATE

Photo courtesy of the National Rural Electric Cooperative Association.

That Wonderful Delco Light Plant

By William H. Ellis

Editor's Note: From the building of huge hydroelectric dams to power rural electrification through such monoliths as the Tennessee Valley Authority, let's not forget the industrious small-time farmer looking for a way to power up before the power lines made it to his acreage.—KT

In April 1933, I was laid off from my job as a clerk in a small-town grocery store in Kentucky. My salary was only $30 per month, but business was so bad that the storeowner could no longer afford to keep two clerks. Since at age 26 I was the youngest, I was the unlucky one, and I found myself without a job. My expenses were nominal, however, as I was single and living at home with my parents on a small farm.

But I didn't like to be idle for long. Since I had some mechanical knowledge of automobiles, a few wrenches and other hand tools, I began doing repair work on cars. For $5 I bought a secondhand Delco Farm Electric Plant. In my shop, which I set up under a large oak tree in my parents' front yard, I repaired this engine and generator. I bought five six-volt car batteries, which, by connecting them in series, equaled 30 volts. I then connected the batteries to the electric plant. I bought these storage batteries at the wholesale price of $7.95 each.

The Delco Farm Electric System was 850 watts; it would light seventeen 50-watt light bulbs, enough for most any small farm. I wired my parents' house with open knob and tube wiring and put one light in each room. I put a plug-in receptacle in the living room for a 32-volt radio and another in the kitchen where Mother could plug in a 32-volt electric iron. Each light had a chain-pull socket to turn it on and off. When we left one room, we turned off the light to save the batteries and turned on the

light in the next room. We thought we were really uptown since we were the only family within miles who had electricity.

The electric plant was installed in the smokehouse and my father or one of us three boys tended to it. The system started on gasoline by priming it with a squirt can, and when the engine warmed up in about a minute, it would run on kerosene (or coal oil). Our electric lights, radio and electric iron cost us about 75 cents per month to operate.

One of us menfolk started this Delco engine early on Friday morning, Mother's ironing day. She did her ironing while the batteries got enough charge to run the radio and electric lights until the next Friday. The engine burned about two gallons of kerosene each Friday at a cost of 10 cents per gallon. And about every three months, we changed the lubricating oil at a cost of 20 cents.

My oldest sister and her husband had a small daughter, Lavonne, barely 3 years of age. One day, when all the menfolk were working in the field and Mother was busy cooking dinner, she suddenly heard the Delco engine start. Mother thought that Lavonne was playing in the yard. Mother immediately went to the back door and called Lavonne, who came to the door of the smokehouse and answered her. Mother ran out to see what she was up to and asked her what she was doing in there.

The little lady said she had just started the engine. Mother said, "Lordy, you have got this thing started and I don't know how to stop it."

Lavonne said, "I can stop it," and reaching over, she tripped the relay and the engine stopped. The child had seen one of the men start the engine so many times that she knew as much about it as we did. You can bet that Mother took the little lady out of the smokehouse and locked the door. ✮

Those "Nothing Special" Inventions

By Richard Bauman

You hop out of bed and your feet sink into nylon carpeting. Perhaps your breakfast eggs are cooked in a Teflon-coated frying pan. Driving to work, drops of rain on the windshield are whisked away by windshield wipers. At work you swig a cup of coffee made in a drip coffeemaker—or maybe you prefer tea, made with a tea bag, of course.

Our lives revolve around "everyday" inventions: commonplace things we either can't or won't do without. Some were the result of creative determination, but many of these items were the result of chance happenings.

★ ★ ★ ★ ★

Frank Epperson "invented" something really "cool"—the Popsicle. And he was just 11 years old at the time. He had made a glass of lemonade, then became distracted and left it, stir-stick and all, sitting on his back porch. That night in 1905, the thermometer plunged below freezing. The next morning Frank found his lemonade frozen on the stick. Epperson didn't do anything with the idea for eight years. Then, remembering the frozen glob of lemonade, he patented it as "frozen fruit water on a stick."

The unique "twin-stick" Popsicle was also Epperson's idea. During the Great Depression of the 1930s, when businesses were reeling and sales were disappearing, Epperson figured he could still sell Popsicles by either giving consumers more for their money or making them feel like they were getting a bargain. The twin-stick Popsicle did both. A parent could buy one Popsicle, split it evenly, and make two kids happy for the price of one.

★ ★ ★ ★ ★

Thomas Edison invented the electric light bulb, but who invented the process of frosting light-bulb glass on the inside?

In the early 1930s, manufacturers knew that light bulbs frosted on the inside were better. They also knew it was impossible to do on a production-line basis. In fact, a popular prank at General Electric Corp. was to tell a newly hired engineer that his first assignment was to frost bulbs on the inside. After a few days, the new

hire would be let in on the joke and everybody would have a good laugh.

Marvin Pipkin, though, took the task seriously. He experimented with acids until he came up with a mixture that swiftly and uniformly attacked the glass. Then he developed ways to use his chemicals on a production-line basis, and changed the way light bulbs are made.

★ ★ ★ ★ ★

Early in 1904, tea merchant Thomas Sullivan sent out samples of new teas to his customers. Many of his customers who had enthusiastically ordered teas now were returning their purchases, complaining about the way they were packed.

To economize, Sullivan's tea samples were packaged in small silk bags rather than in tins. Most of his customers had left the tea in the bags when they brewed it. The bags were convenient, and they expected their tea to be packaged that way. To accommodate them, Sullivan experimented with various materials to use for tea bags. Silk was too expensive. He found a cheap gauze worked best. Thus, the tea bag was invented.

★ ★ ★ ★ ★

King Camp Gillette wanted to invent something that a person would use once, toss away and then buy another again—and again and again. He considered various products until he was shaving one morning in 1892. His old straight razor was dull and needed a professional honing. "As I stood in front of the mirror, razor in hand, I saw it," claimed Gillette. "I had the idea for inexpensive, thin steel blades, sharpened on two edges." His idea was a good one, but it took him 11 frustrating years to develop the process for making ultra-thin blades.

In December 1903, the Gillette Safety Razor Co. sold 50 razors. A year later, more than 90,000 razors were sold. By 1905, men had bought over a quarter-million razors and blades.

★ ★ ★ ★ ★

"We weren't trying to create a fiber, we were doing basic research on polymers. At the time we had no end use in mind at all," said

Thomas Edison, Henry Ford, and Francis Jehl recreating the invention of the incandescent light bulb, 1929. Marvin Pipkin added frosting to the inside of the bulb years later. From the Collections of Henry Ford Museum and Greenfield Village.

Dr. Julian W. Hill, who, in 1930, created strands of a taffylike material in his laboratory. It was the forerunner of nylon.

Fifty years ago, magazine ads proclaimed nylon to be a great advancement into the world of tomorrow. How prophetic! Nylon stockings were the first consumer application of the fiber. In 1938, scientists at Du Pont started using nylon fibers as toothbrush bristles.

Then someone got the idea that nylon could be formed into thin, threadlike fibers, and woven into nylon fabric usable for stockings. Although more expensive than the silk stockings they replaced, women were promised that the stockings were practically indestructible. It was an exaggeration, to be sure, when they first went on sale in May 1940.

Nevertheless, women stood in block-long lines, eager to pay $1.50 a pair for the revolutionary hose. By the end of the 1940s, nylon was being used in carpeting, upholstery and dozens of other consumer products. It is the most popular carpeting fiber today.

⋆⋆⋆⋆⋆

While scientists in one part of Du Pont were experimenting with nylon in 1938, another Du Pont scientist, Roy Plunkett, was trying to find a new refrigerant gas. The result of his experiments was a marvelous substance—Teflon.

"Teflon was truly an accident," says Dave Jones, Du Pont's Teflon development manager.

One of the compounds Plunkett experimented with was tetrafluoroethylene gas. When all the gas escaped from its container during a failed experiment, the residue left behind was a white, waxy material. Others might have tossed it out, but Plunkett was intrigued. He ran tests on the material and said of that substance: "[It] was virtually inert to all known solvents, acids and bases. I realized we had stumbled onto a unique and unusual material." Teflon had the lowest coefficient of friction of any known solid material. It was secret World War II material.

⋆⋆⋆⋆⋆

The health of trolley-car motormen inspired Mary Anderson to invent windshield wipers. Miss Anderson, of Elmwood, Ala., worried that streetcar motormen would catch cold or pneumonia during rainstorms. They commonly got soaked cleaning rain from the windshields of their trolleys with a rag.

The basic design for the windshield wiper came easily, but virtually every engineer she talked to told her the idea wouldn't work. Undaunted, she made the prototype herself. In November 1903, she received a patent for her first hand-operated windshield wiper. After that, motormen and eventually motorists stayed dry even in the worst storms and still saw clearly.

⋆⋆⋆⋆⋆

William Addis wasn't a typical inventor. He was a criminal. In 1790 he was convicted of inciting a riot, and was incarcerated at Newgate Prison in London. While brushes were nothing new, using one to clean one's teeth was unheard of. Instead, a piece of cloth or natural sponge and salt were typically used to clean teeth.

When the idea of a toothbrush came to him, Addis carved a piece of bone into a form somewhat like today's toothbrushes. At one end he laboriously hewed several small holes. Then he tied bristles from an old scrub brush (probably hog hair) into small bundles and secured them in the tiny holes. His toothbrush worked remarkably well.

Addis reworked the design dozens of times. When he got out of prison he started a business supplying wealthy Britons with his newfangled toothbrushes.

⋆⋆⋆⋆⋆

Did you have a cup of coffee this morning? Was the coffee made with a drip coffeemaker? If so, you used Melitta Bentz's idea for making better coffee.

In 1908, when Mrs. Bentz of Dresden, Germany, decided there had to be a better way to make coffee than wrapping it in a cloth and boiling it, the result of which was bitter coffee.

She reasoned that better-tasting coffee could be made by pouring boiling water through the ground beans. She punched holes in the bottom of an old metal pot and covered the holes with a disk cut from blotter paper. She added a few scoops of coffee, and when she poured boiling water through it, it made extraordinarily good coffee.

Melitta and her husband, Hugo, made up dozens of "coffeemakers" as she called them, and took them to the Leipzig Trade Fair in 1909. She received orders for more than 1,200 of them.

So, you see, nearly everything we use at work, home and for leisure activities was invented by someone who had an idea, and pursued it faithfully to the end. ⋆

The Hackney Auto Plow

By Lucille Howe

*I*f you happen to be near my age—I was born in 1900—and if you spent your youth in the Midwest, especially if you lived on a farm, you may have seen one. If you did, you have the advantage over me. Even though three of my uncles invented, manufactured and sold the Hackney Auto Plow, I never had a close look at one until 1967, when it had become a collector's item.

The uncles were my mother's brothers, Leslie, William and Joseph Hackney, better known to many by their initials. Even their parents and their six sisters usually referred to them at L.S., W.L. and J.M.

The brothers' first business venture was as land brokers. They made themselves each a nice nest egg, the largest profits resulting from the buying and selling of railroad land in North Dakota. The government granted huge tracts of land there to railroad companies to encourage the building of new roads. In the early years of the 20th century, much of this land was available at very low prices. It was also sold at nominal prices, but the turnover was enormous.

It was probably while the brothers were in the Dakotas promoting land sales that they saw the need for some power other than that of teams of many horses, or big steam rigs, to break the prairie and work the large fields.

L.S. and W.L. were already inventors of sorts. I have seen the patent papers, long

1912 Hackney Auto Plow on display at the Dale and Martha Hawk Museum, Wolford, N.D. Photo courtesy of Randy Hackney.

outdated, for a device L.S. invented to easily grease and clean underneath a car. His frame held the car and tipped it on its side. Apparently, a grease pit is more practical.

I was fascinated by the working model of a gate opener and closer W.L. invented. It was no electronic device; just a simple combination of ropes and pulleys. But with it, a person could open and close the gate without getting out of his carriage or car.

L.S. and W.L. pooled their talents and came up with the plow to which they gave the family name. It was not a tractor to pull a plow, but a mechanized plow. They built a factory. J.M. came in as a member of the Hackney Manufacturing Co. and in 1912, they were in business.

For a few years they sold a considerable number of the plows. Their largest sales were in the Dakotas and Minnesota, but they also sold the plows in other parts of the country and even some abroad. Things looked very promising.

But trouble loomed. The plow did not always perform as well as the advertising promised. More and more good pull-type tractors were being developed. Sales declined. When the factory burned to the ground, the company folded. Grandpa said, "If the boys had only got the bugs out of the machine, it might have been a success."

Whether it was "bugs," competition or mismanagement, the plow was manufactured for only a few years in the factory at Prior and University in St. Paul, Minn. For some time, the lot where the factory had stood was covered with unsold plows. It was there that I finally got a glimpse of them now and then from a streetcar window when I attended college in St. Paul.

As young people, we had heard a good deal about the plow Mother's brothers had invented. We heard that a couple had been sold in our county. One of my brothers remembers being allowed to sit on one when it was being demonstrated in our town. But as the years passed, the plow was mentioned less and less when the family got together.

Then, as my brothers and sisters and I grew older, we began to go back farther and farther in memory, and wondered about our uncles' invention. Might there be one still in existence somewhere? One sister took up the question in earnest, and after looking over many engine magazines and corresponding with many gas engine buffs, she found a collector in North Dakota who had one in such good condition that he had recently driven it in a parade. She wrote to him and got permission for some of us to go see it.

Thus it was that in the summer of 1967, my sister, my brother and I found ourselves in the presence of a memory come to life. My first impression was of its great size. From the streetcar window, the machines had looked much smaller. It looked as new as if it had just come from the factory; the paint was bright, the plow shiny. The owner of the Hackney, who also owned a seemingly endless selection of other old tractors and machines of all sorts, explained that it had been in a shed with door and

The Hackney brothers, Joseph, William and Leslie were the inventors of the Hackney Auto Plow. Photo courtesy of Randy Hackney, great-great-grandson of Leslie Hackney.

windows boarded shut for many years. A widow who was liquidating her estate had sold it to him. The collector called it his most prized possession.

The widow also gave him the manual that had come with it from the factory, so he was able to paint it as it had been originally. In that manual we found a picture of W.L. in a group watching the plow at work.

The kind collector drove the plow out into the yard so we could take pictures of it and see it move. My brother drove it, and we all discovered a couple of things about it that we hadn't known. For one thing, it had a hitch so it could pull machinery. I wondered if the inventors had visions of it pulling a disk or harrow as it plowed. I'm afraid it didn't have the power for both.

Its second peculiarity was that it could be driven two ways forward. If you were heading south and wanted to turn north, you manipulated a lever and moved from the seat you had been using to one facing it, and away you went in the opposite direction.

The Hackney Auto Plow was one example of American ingenuity, even if it was short-lived. I'm proud to have my name stamped on one of the inventions that helped make this nation great. ✮

Harnessing the Wind

By Marge Lifto as told to Claus Bienhoff

In the 1870s, Henry Emminga decided to build a large prairie mill in his hometown of Keokuk Junction, Ill. (renamed Golden in 1880). A skilled mechanic and mill-wright, he went out into the oak, maple and hickory forests to cut the lumber. With his brawn and brains, plus the cooperation of carpenters in town, he set up the windmill, piece by piece.

Its first story was completed within a few months. During the following winter and spring, Emminga hand-carved the wooden parts for the machinery. He used hard maple for the master wheel, which measured 12 feet in diameter. This piece alone took eight months to finish. Additional stories were then added, until the mill stood 92 feet high.

Built like a typical European mill, its broad base narrowed as it reached the tower. The tower housed the vertical shaft, the only major part of the machinery made of cast iron. It weighed 5,000 pounds. Fastened to the shaft was the fan, with four blades acting as the wind wheel. These blades had to be assembled on the ground and then hoisted over the cat-walk. From tip to tip, they measured 71 feet and produced 75 horsepower for grinding.

Canvas covered the blades, to catch the wind

After much restoration, the Golden Prairie Mills Windmill is once again grinding wheat. Photos courtesy of the Golden (Ill.) Historical Society.

like a sail. When the wind grew too strong, these sails were rolled up and the shutters on the blades were opened to let the wind through. When there was no wind, volunteers from town worked 24-hour shifts to operate the mill manually.

Emminga had the support of the community behind him. With broadax and crosscut saw, these men hewed and carved the wood until all the gears and cogwheels were finished.

Two big stone wheels, flat sides together, formed a set. There were three sets of burr wheels, called millstones, which did the grinding. One might weigh 4,000–5,000 pounds and could grind as much as 500 bushels of grain a day. A spider wheel and wench-type contraption put the mill into action. There was a crucial need for flour then, not only for the surrounding area but also for parts of Europe. (After World War I, flour was scarce, and buckwheat, graham and rye flours, and cornmeal were made here.)

Building the large mill pieces called for huge amounts of material that were not always available locally, so neighborhood farmers hauled wagonloads of rocks from nearby creeks. Horses and wagons also carried the grain from the elevator to the mill, where it became flour. Then it was taken to the grain cars on the tracks. It rode the rails for hundreds of miles before reaching the coast, where it was loaded onto ships bound for other countries.

The horses often balked and ran off when they were frightened by the huge moving shadows made by the blades as they turned. However, in 1924, a violent storm badly damaged the windmill's wings. That's when the 30-horsepower gasoline engine came into use. It just wasn't quite the same after that.

But today a civic project to restore the prairie mill in Golden has been underway. The huge blades of Henry Emminga's mill again slowly turn, harnessing the wind to grind the grains of life. ☆

The Golden prairie mill was in operation from 1872 through 1924. This photograph was taken about 1900.

The steel industry was the backbone of many "Rust Belt" cities for over a century. This mural of a blast furnace in Portsmouth, Ohio, was painted by artist Robert Dafford on the city's flood wall.

The Backbone of Our Town

By Anne Pierre Spangler

Editor's Note: How could we discuss the building of a nation without mentioning the steel industry and its hardworking men and women? I had an uncle, Arthur Kelley, who worked in the Sheffield Steel plant of Kansas City, and his stories of the industry filled my young mind with images of steelworkers forging the metal that made our country grow.—KT

Today, the sprawling industrial complex comprised of several city blocks called Bethlehem Steel lies silent, a haunting reminder of past prosperity. After a sale of parts that brought curious buyers from all over the world, the property itself is up for sale. Since the early 1900s, the welfare of Lebanon, Pa.,—my hometown—hinged mostly on the ups and downs of the steel industry. Now, it must search for new resources if it is to be saved at all.

A smaller concern, Lebanon Steel Foundry, is still operating on a small scale after many setbacks, including a long, crippling strike. It was started in 1911 by two Englishmen, William H. Worrilow and Thomas S. Quinn. It became a family affair, with their sons continuing the business.

In 1917, Bethlehem Steel moved into our area after merging with the iron and steel interest left by the affluent Coleman family, who also had emigrated from England. Our plants were some of the first to be converted to defense production prior to World War II. Lebanon Steel received both Army and Navy "E" Awards, in addition to two subsequent awards. Circle-L Steel Castings, as they were eventually called, evoked pride in our town as they entered into useful purposes on land, at sea and in the air. They were used in railroads in our country and elsewhere. Several continents reaped the benefits of our hard workers.

Paul Spangler remembers the boomtown that once was Lebanon, Pa. He was born here in 1913 and has lived here all of his life, never tempted to leave. After World War I, when a flu epidemic ravaged our country, David Spangler, Paul's father, was a victim. He had made a good living for his family at Bethlehem Steel, but it was difficult to maintain his strength after losing a lung. He remained frail until his death when Paul was quite small.

Besides Paul, a middle child, there were Raymond, Peter and Dorothy. Agnes, their widowed mother, became so desperate at one point that she decided to put the children in an orphanage. But the morning that they were scrubbed and polished, ready to go, she broke down and relented. She would manage some way.

She secured a job at the Bethlehem Steel Plant where her husband had been employed. In those days, women were not allowed to do a man's work, so she examined work and did paperwork. She worked long hours. The Spangler children became latchkey kids, fending for themselves quite a bit, which only contributed to their independence.

Throughout the nationwide Depression, our steel industry kept our heads above water. Then the unthinkable happened. The steel mill closed. They said it could not happen, but it did—and our people are still in a state of shock. We have only memories left of those Good Old Days. ✩

A Giant Remembered

By Alan Sanderson

Giant. No other word could be used to describe the sprawling textile complex called the Esmond Mills. They dominated Esmond, R.I., the village that grew up around them and because of them, and in the process became the financial foundation on which I and many of my friends were raised. Thanks to good management, workmanship and a wartime government contract, the excellent quality of Esmond "Bunny Blankets" became known throughout the country.

Clocks were regularly wound and set to the shrill blasts of the noon and 3 o'clock whistles. By them I could always tell when I should start home from my play. Others of my generation headed toward brick houses adjoining the main road that had originally been built for mill workers.

It was here that my dad, Thomas Sanderson, obtained his first job upon landing on these shores in 1930. The Great Depression had a stranglehold on the wheels of industry then, and he was limited to a few days' work at a stretch. Nevertheless, he was glad even of this, because it was more than any other shop or factory was offering.

But with the dawn of the Roosevelt era, conditions slowly improved. Workers came to appreciate a full week's earnings, though they endured 12-hour shifts. Never one to be content with what he'd already achieved, my dad would tell anyone who cared to listen that someday he himself would oversee Esmond's complete dyeing operation. Within 15 years, through pure hard work and gritty determination, darned if he

didn't! In that period he also became co-inventor of a revolutionary continuous dyeing machine that bore an imprint of his name.

For all these accomplishments, however, there remains one touch of irony that cannot be omitted. He once confessed to me that, as a youth in his native England, he'd disliked the textile business so much that he'd come to the United States to avoid being caught up in it!

I, therefore, came to hear of the mill quite naturally while growing up. Many a conversation passed between my parents regarding the everyday problems my dad faced, particularly when he'd gained a position of responsibility.

This smoke-stacked beehive of activity sat about a mile from where we lived. On special days I was awarded the privilege of bringing my dad's lunch to him. It was quite a treat for me and it wouldn't have done to be late with it. Whether boss or laborer, fresh or tired, busy or relaxed, when that noon whistle let loose its customary shriek, my dad would stop to eat his three sandwiches. He'd wait for me by the main gate and I'd join him in a bite.

If he could spare a few minutes more, I'd be shown through his department and others. Thus, at a very early age, I became acquainted with the deafening clack of the looms in the weave room, the slopping swish of cloth being run in the big dye house kettles, and the strong, distinctive smell of fabric being processed. Here and there I'd be introduced to workers busy at their machines.

While my dad looked on, they treated me with the greatest deference (or so it seemed to me) as they tried to explain how their napping machine put fuzz on blankets

> *As a youth in his native England, he'd disliked the textile business so much that he'd come to the United States to avoid being caught up in it!*

or how goods were inspected for knots in the burling department.

Thoughts of such special treatment helped sustain me when the time came for me to leave my dad. He'd pass me through the gate and then issue a final wave from just inside the door to the plant. Then I'd skip merrily home, filled with hopes that my next visit wasn't too far off.

Since wages and benefits generously topped working conditions elsewhere, it was inevitable that I should begin my working life at the Esmond Mills. When school recessed for the summer of 1947, I passed my first physical exam and was immediately hired. Next to the roar of the carding machinery and shut off by a sliding door was the relatively quiet little nook called the "picker room" to which I was assigned. In addition to making the roaming caterer a good deal richer, my duties included straightening balling wires by guiding them through a tool composed mainly of two heavy adjoining wheels, and trucking waste outside. I hardly ever missed an opportunity to remove the trash because my travels led me to where I could experience a new phenomenon, passing through an electric-eye door.

The first wages I received were from a guarded paymaster who distributed pay envelopes to the employees of each room. My earnings were the glory of my young life.

In September, when my senior year rolled around at school, I was able to secure employment on the night shift. My job, which I thoroughly enjoyed, was much different in the "piece dye" department, which was then mostly engaged in bleaching cotton. This was done in "jigs," or large vats, over which were suspended two large wooden rollers. Cloth wound on one of these rollers from a selected truck was mechanically lowered into various solutions below and rewound on the opposite cylinder. Back and forth the ordered cloth was made to go to complete specified running times, ranging

This smoke-stacked beehive of activity sat about a mile from where we lived. On special days I was awarded the privilege of bringing my dad's lunch to him.

from two hours to just four "ends."

Caustic soda from a barrel had to be handled with gloves and goggles, bleach and acids were among the ingredients dissolved in different refills of water. "Leaders" (short lengths of rejected cloth) were sewn to both ends to insure treatment of the entire bolt. These leaders were also necessary to know when the jig should be stopped so that the turning of the overhead rollers could be reversed. It was no fun fishing around for a lost end with a large iron hook. Something less could be said of getting splashed while reattaching it to its rightful place.

Two men had five jigs to operate between them on each of the three eight-hour shifts. After every load of cotton had been put through its paces, I'd end my association with it by testing the finished product for any trace of unwanted chemicals. Then I'd wheel it out to a gigantic metal enclosure called the dryer.

After graduation from high school, I returned to day work, but this was 1948, an era of diminished consumer demands and soaring labor costs. Accordingly, things were not good at Esmond Mills. Management and union representatives could not come to terms. Eventually, the owner decided he had no other alternative than to close his doors forever. A giant had been sent toppling, and hundreds of people, some of them with lifetimes of seniority, suddenly found themselves out on the street.

It was the beginning of the end of the textile industry in Rhode Island. Other mills followed suit or moved south, where business costs were considerably cheaper.

Our locale is the poorer for it, but the now-rented buildings still stand in their entirety, a testimonial to the great firm they once housed. Pointed out to strangers as the "old Esmond Mills," their place as the village landmark is as secure as ever. As I gaze in its direction in a nostalgic frame of mind, I can almost hear that whistle blow. ✯

Pullman-Standard As I Saw It

By Charles Bundo Jr.

When my mother's brother, Uncle Walt Little, advised me to go by the Pullman-Standard Engineering Department for an interview with Dick Cunningham, their chief draftsman, I jumped at the chance. At the time I was employed in a brass foundry, grinding rough spots off new castings—a very disagreeable job in an oven-hot, smoke-filled, factory room. The year was 1937, in Chicago.

Uncle Walt was a career Pullman employee—a fixture in the accounting department. It was very kind of him to arrange the unsolicited opportunity for an interview, especially since he had a rather unenthusiastic opinion of me. Mostly he did it because of my mother.

During my interview, I found out that in addition to Uncle Walt's sponsorship, I had another element in my favor. In 1932, I had attended Pullman Technical High School for one year. It was a privately endowed school on the level of a modern vocational school. Prospective students had to be close relatives of a Pullman employee, who in turn had to sponsor them. Long ago, Uncle Walt had also done that for me.

At Pullman Tech I had opted for engineering. This school dispensed with fancy educational subjects and concentrated on the matter at hand. Engineering meant four hours a day at drafting, one hour on English thrice per week, and a steady daily hour of mathematics. It was darned good training, and, provided one could survive the four-year course, a Pullman job was assured after graduation.

So I was hired for the engineering department "blueprint vault," which contained all the drawings produced by the department, contemporaneous or from bygone times. Some of the recent drawings were in constant demand for reference use by the drafting staff of more than 100.

I was low man on the tall totem pole. Two much younger chaps also worked in the blueprint vault, and we were kept busy all day filling orders and refiling drawings that were returned. This job paid $75 a month—for 44 hours per week—with paydays twice each month. Promotion from the vault to a drawing board was strictly on a seniority basis; the two lads already in the vault had to move out before I could. And their movement depended upon attrition in the drafting room—retirements, deaths, very occasional transfers out and, just as rare, resignations. It seems no one ever was fired. Already in the drafting room were several of my old Pullman Tech classmates who had gone all the way.

The Pullman Administration Building with its clock tower is pictured in the factory complex.

Pullman Market Hall (below left) and Arcade Building (below right) as they appeared in the 1890s. All photographs courtesy the Historic Pullman Foundation Archives.

had the only bar in town. And there was an outdoor-indoor marketplace, a forerunner of today's supermarkets.

Pullman, founder of the Pullman Palace Car Co. in 1867, created the town of Pullman, the first planned model industrial town. In early 1880, George Pullman purchased nearly 4,000 acres just west of Lake Calumet and surrounding the Illinois Central Railroad, to build his model town in 1880.

The engineering department was housed on the top floor of the Pullman Administration Building, which featured a clock tower, and was adjacent to 111th Street on Cottage Grove Avenue in Chicago. This top floor was partially roofed with corrugated tin. It was cold and barnlike in winter, and a sweatbox hellhole in summer. All the draftsmen wore cloth wrappings on their arms to keep sweat off their drawings on the warmest days.

I lived a 20-minute streetcar ride away from work, but most of the engineering personnel lived in nearby Roseland, a community spawned by and economically supported by Pullman workers. Most of them walked many blocks to work, rain or shine. Their family cars appeared only on Saturdays, when we worked the four-hour last stint of the week. The cars were neat, always shiny, and as well kept as their Roseland homes and stores.

George M. Pullman had built an entire town for his shop and labor force—street after street lined with look-alike townhouses. Office personnel preferred to live off the premises. The town even had its own hotel, the once-gracious Florence, now somewhat faded and with no transient guests. Old retired shop workers live there. The Florence Hotel also

Most of the town of Pullman was built between 1880–84, by architect Solon Beman and landscape architect Nathan Barrett. The center of town was the railroad car business. A clock tower dominated the large industrial complex. The housing was well-constructed with many "modern" conveniences for 1880s standards such as indoor plumbing, sewage and a gas works. The parks and streets were pleasantly landscaped. The town would not be complete without public facilities such as stores and office buildings. A bank, library, theatre, post office, church, parks and recreational facilities were provided as part of the town.

In 1896, Pullman was presented an award for "The World's Most Perfect Town." The town prospered for fourteen years until the depression of 1893, about the time of the Chicago World's Fair.

To keep his business open, Pullman reduced wages and hours, which resulted in the famous Pullman Strike of 1894. Pullman died in 1897.

George M. Pullman (above) was the father of the Pullman empire. Above right: a certificate of Pullman Co. stock. Photos courtesy the Historic Pullman Foundation Archives.

and finished drawings were made on pencil-type linen and later traced in ink for final records. I was a pretty darned good draftsman!

Career progress at Pullman was usually pretty slow. However, mostly because of the quality of my work, plus a small application of office politics, I progressed from engineering and draftsman to the very elite Color and Design Department. The quarters were separate from, but adjoining, engineering. Here I functioned comfortably until early 1940, when I left for more lucrative employment in a West Coast aircraft engineering department.

Always I shall remember Pullman as a great training ground for aspiring draftsmen and designers. Their standards were second to none. It was a formative time for me, and the values I fortunately assimilated then have served me well. ☆

In 1898 an Illinois Supreme Court ruling required the company to sell its nonindustrial property.

The housing was all sold by 1907 and has been privately owned ever since. The City of Chicago annexed the town of Pullman along with Hyde Park Township in 1889. When the nonindustrial property was sold, the rest of the parks, streets and the school system were taken over by Chicago allowing Pullman to become just another neighborhood.

The predominant ethnic flavor in all Pullman departments and shops were Dutch. George M. Pullman had imported a series of Dutch immigrants as the nucleus of his workforce. These men—or mostly their descendants, by my time— were scattered throughout the enterprise. Mr. Pullman had good respect for the dependability, expertise and good nature of Dutch workers. The gamble had paid off very well for him. These were good men, all with strange-sounding names that usually ended with "stra" or "sma."

I spent almost a year in the blueprint vault before I graduated to a board in the Interiors Group in the drawing room. School and some practice of my own volition had readied me for tasks in this uncomplicated drawing group. My work was always flawlessly neat and legible. Before long, I began to get the almost "picture type," general-assembly drawing assignments, which were made on very large sheets. All final

Some of the rowhouses Pullman provided for company housing have now been restored. This recent photograph by Ned Rissky courtesy the Historic Pullman Foundation Archives.

Grasshopper Oil Strike

By Olive W. Freeman

I grew up in a western Pennsylvania town where the hillsides were dotted with oil derricks. Oil and lumber had drawn the early settlers, and in Warren, Pa., refining oil was a major business.

Here, in oil country, it seemed as if people we knew were always either "hitting a gusher" or "bringing in a dry hole." When the latter happened, one of my little friends would vanish from school while her family went "to live on the lease" until matters improved and they could return to their house on Market Street.

I don't imagine that many of us grew up there without seeing an oil well "shot off." We'd watch as the go-devil was dropped down it, then wait breathlessly for the resulting spectacular explosion.

And I'll never forget the awesome but gorgeous blaze that resulted when a refinery oil-storage tank was hit by a lightning bolt. It seemed the whole town turned out, even though it was the middle of the night. We knew it meant a dreadful loss for someone, but we had to exult in the glorious colors of those flames against the sky's blackness.

The area around the refineries was called "The Flats," and it was there that the refinery workers had built their simple homes. During the hot summer of 1905, one of those workers, John Larson, put down a water well with a pitcher pump. One day soon thereafter, his son pumped up more than water—a thick, dark liquid. He collected a sample in a bottle and rushed it three blocks to the Seneca Oil works, where a friendly chemist reported it crude oil with very little water. When he took the news to his father, John Larson, without a word to anyone, put down seven more wells with pitcher pumps on his property, and began selling his oil at $1.87 a barrel.

Of course, the operation couldn't be hidden. A neighbor, Charles Haggstrom, saw what was going on and promptly put down a well inside his house. When his well also brought up oil, the news couldn't be kept under wraps.

On Aug. 22, the newspaper shouted it out in headlines. Crowds of Warrenites hurried to the neighborhood of Carver and Irvine Streets. If manna had fallen from heaven, Warren might not have known what to do with it, but everyone knew what to do with oil: Get it out of the ground, and turn it into money.

As the crowds saw what was happening, land in the area was frantically bought or leased by all sorts of people, from legitimate businessmen to young boys, and wells went down. By that night, you couldn't buy a pitcher pump anywhere.

Two boys I knew in school, Earl Dunkle and his brother, fenced their small lease with chicken wire and proudly put up their sign for "The Hen Coop Oil Co."

All those little pumps going up and down sounded like a horde of grasshoppers. Newspaper accounts began to speak of "The Grasshopper Oil Strike," and they reported daily progress.

Oil was found no deeper than 15–25 feet below the surface and, since the first few days showed that it came from a narrow strip of land, the most acceptable theory was that it was the result of seepage from the refineries, or possibly from a pipeline leak. Meanwhile, the pumps were bringing up about 50 barrels a day, and most of it was sold promptly to the Wilburine Oil Co.

By October, the beautiful, dark oil had disappeared. The pitcher pumps were gone, too, and the shrill piping of real grasshoppers at last could be heard.

No fortunes were made or lost, but here and there a mortgage was paid off, or a child helped to further his education. Once again, my town had found out that there's more than money in oil. Even a little "strike" could entertain and delight the whole community. ✪

Wyoming Oil Fields

By Fred Droddy

When my father-in-law left the gold mines in Lead City, S.D., he moved to Casper, Wyo., and found work at an oil refinery. In the 1920s, Wyoming oil fields were booming and employment could be had by anyone who was willing to work.

There was no organized labor there at the time, and my father-in-law was instrumental in helping organize the Pipe Fitters Union in Casper. He became quite involved in union business during the three or four years he worked at the refinery. This didn't make him too popular with the refinery management, and they put him on all the miserable jobs they could find. He finally quit and went out in the oil fields to work.

He has been gone for many years, but while he was still alive, he told me what it was like to work in the Wyoming oil fields back then, in the 1920s. It was a tough, dirty job. The winters were cold and snowy, and the summers were hot and dusty. The wind seemed to blow constantly, winter and summer. There was nothing to stop it for miles. In the summer, the wind deposited the fine prairie dust in every crack and cranny; in the winter, it piled the snow in drifts 10–12 feet deep in the hollows and scoured it off the higher ground. When spring's warmer temperatures melted the snow, the fields became big mud holes.

The Salt Creek Oil Field, approximately 50 miles north of Casper, was no different from others situated in a barren wasteland. But although this land looked barren on the surface, deep underneath was a fortune in black gold just waiting to be tapped.

When oil was first struck there, camps sprang up to accommodate the influx of workers, and these settlements evolved into thriving communities. Bunkhouses were built for the single men, as were boardinghouses, and rental housing for men with families.

These rentals were similar, varying only in size; the larger the family, the larger the rental they needed. Each had a detached garage in back, and the company furnished heat and electricity for both house and garage. A heated garage was a necessity if you wished to start your car in the wintertime.

The only modern plumbing in these rentals was a kitchen sink with cold running water. There was no hot water for dishes, bathing or anything else; water had to be heated on the cookstove for these chores. Nor was the water from the tap potable; it could be used only for bathing, washing clothes and dishes, and scrubbing floors.

Drinking water had to be distilled. The oil company did this at a company-owned distillery adjoining the steam plant. The distilled water was then stored in a central tank, and from there, each family carried or hauled drinkable water.

There were no indoor toilets or bathtubs. People bathed in a galvanized washtub using water heated on the kitchen stove. Nature's call meant a trip out back by the garage to the two-holer. These trips weren't so bad in the summer, but in the winter, when the thermometer dropped to zero and lower, a person postponed the trip as long as possible.

Although these houses were very comfortable in the winter with free gas heat, they could be unbearably hot when summer brought the mercury up to 100 degrees and sometimes more. There was no air conditioning, no trees for shade. Only a forest of oil derricks dotted the landscape, reaching to the horizon.

The clothes the men wore to work the oil rigs became heavily coated with crude oil, and it was next to impossible to wash it out at home. But the company had a way of steaming it out at the steam plant. This was one of the few benefits furnished by the company.

There were no schools in these camps and school buses were unheard of, so children either walked to school or their parents took them. The school nearest Salt Creek was at Midwest, Wyo., approximately two miles away. When it looked like a bad storm or blizzard was in the making, the teacher dismissed classes early so that those who lived some distance away could get home before conditions grew too bad.

High-school students had to wear uniforms—including a white middy, black tie and blue skirt for the girls, white shirt, string tie and pants for the boys. During the cold winter, the students wore dark uniforms, including a navy blue middy for the girls, and flannel or wool shirt for the boys. The teacher designated two special days each school term when the students were allowed to wear clothes of their choice.

The school board formulated these dress policies so that no children would feel inferior because of the way they dressed. Some of the more prosperous families could send their teens to school dressed in a style far beyond what the ordinary working man could afford. These were the families that became rich when oil was found on their property.

In these camps friendships were forged that lasted a lifetime. Even in their retirement years, my in-laws corresponded with friends they had made there in their younger days.

They loved to talk about the good times they had there, about the many friends they met, and about the social

gatherings, picnics, fishing, dances and other entertainment.

There was also the occasional trip into Casper to shop. The 50-mile journey made for a long day with the roads as they were, so such excursions didn't come along too often. It was a gala occasion when they did—unless it rained while one was in town. Then the roads home were almost impassible.

Arriving home late one night after one of these trips to Casper, my father-in-law discovered that a tornado had ripped through part of the oil field, leaving some of the tall derricks in a twisted mass of steel. It had touched down at the edge of camp, and luckily, no one was seriously hurt. But the men had to spend several days cleaning up and replacing the damaged derricks.

Fire was always a hazard with so much crude oil and gas around. It was not unusual for one of the holding sumps to catch fire, and occasionally one of the wells. There were men who specialized in controlling fires in the wells and sometimes they had to be called in from other fields far away.

Soon after the Great Depression of the 1930s began, work slacked off in the oil fields as it did elsewhere. The workers and their families had to move and find other work if they could. My father-in-law and his family moved back to the mines and worked there. When World War II began, he left and got a job in defense work, from which he retired. ☆

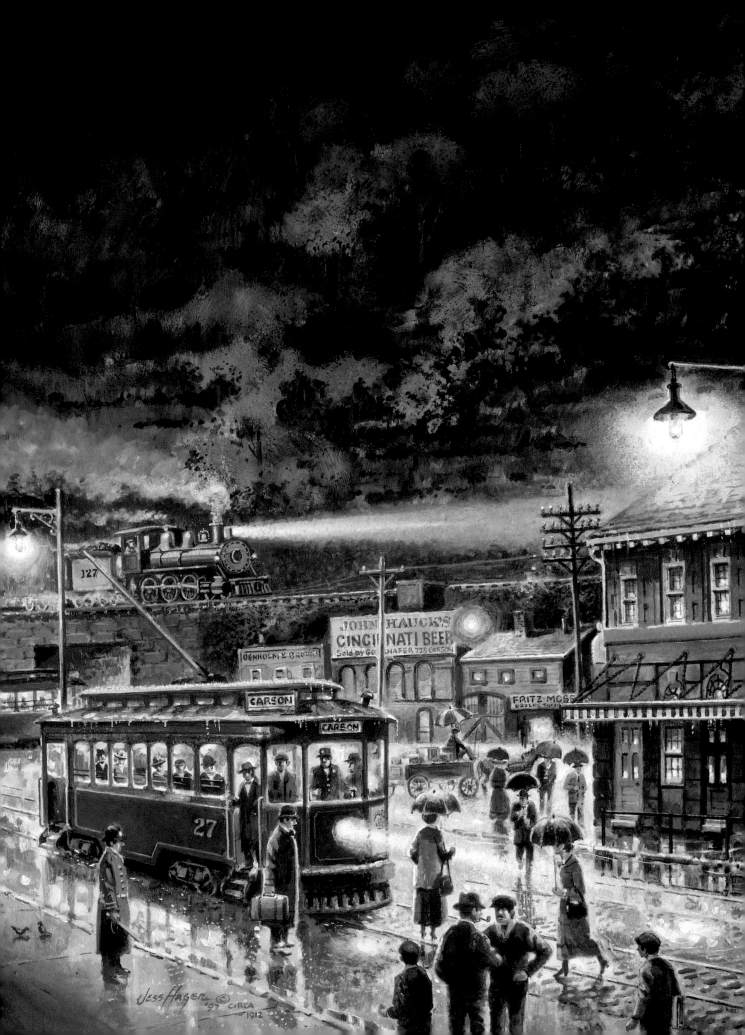

Moving a Nation

Chapter Three

★ ★ ★ ★ ★

When we look at what made this country great, one of the most important elements was the ability to move people and products quickly and efficiently. Think of it. When the 20th century began, automobiles were still more a novelty than a necessity—at least in the eyes of most Americans. Iron horses—the great trains—were still creeping in steam-paced drudgery. The thought of flights crisscrossing our nation's skies was still just a bright Wright dream. But then an innovative people took the dreams of inventors and engineers to their hearts. Instead of getting a horse, they bought Henry Ford's Tin Lizzies by the millions. From the factory to the roads, rails, rivers and skies they moved a nation into the modern era with courage and confidence.

This chapter reminds us of those days in the infancy of modern transportation, when trolleys were the mass transit of choice in most cities. It is dedicated to those people who first envisioned, then built, then used the dream of moving a nation.

—*Ken Tate*

Mr. and Mrs. Henry Ford in the old shop on Bagley Street, Detroit, early in the career of Mr. Ford.

Magic for Rural America

By Patricia Rutherford

Henry Ford made his last Model T in 1927, the year I was born. Our family didn't own one, but I do barely remember them being around. The Model T was the farmer's friend. He used it as a portable power plant. With its rear wheels jacked up and a power takeoff attached, a Ford could saw wood, grind feed and shell corn. It could also plow fields. And after the day's work was done, the family could all load into the machine and go to a movie.

The Model T brought magic to rural America. It was also the doctor's and businessman's car, and was priced low enough that many people could afford it. Good roads hadn't been developed yet, but the Ford could go over any road—or no road at all. In low gear, it could dig its way along through deep mud for mile after mile, its radiator steaming. But the driver had to keep his foot on the pedal all the way, as it was the pressure on this pedal that threw it into low gear.

Ford Motor Co. was established on June 16, 1903, with $150,000 capital. Henry Ford was the president, head of engineering and general manager.

The rattling Model T Ford was sometimes called a jalopy, Tin Lizzie or flivver. Built by Henry Ford between 1908–1927, it was called "the common man's car." It was a unique contributor to the history of transportation.

The Model T had a four-cylinder engine that generated 20 horsepower. It had three-point suspension and an eel-like ability to twist and turn. The Model T was considered sensational when it was introduced. In all, 15,007,033 were built.

The Model T had a personality all its own. We never knew if the engine was going to keep running. Sometimes it wouldn't start on cold mornings. Legend has it that the Model T could go forward and backward at the same time. This seemed to be true because many drivers used reverse as a brake, seemingly shifting the car from forward to backward almost without a pause.

The first Model T's didn't have starters, but were equipped instead with a hand-turned crank out front. Sometimes it kicked back, breaking an arm or a wrist or skinning knuckles.

When the Model T first started, it vibrated, rattled and shook. It was always a race to run and jump into the seat before it sputtered and stalled. At first the engine would hit only on two or three cylinders; the fourth would start firing some seconds later. Only when the oil in the transmission had been thoroughly warmed would old Lizzie settle down and quit shaking.

Model T's had 30-inch wheels, equipped with 3-inch tires on the front and 3½-inch tires on the back. Most Model-T tires were solid rubber.

Fuel was fed by gravity from a tank under the seat. The passenger had to get out of the car when it was being filled with fuel. There was no gas gauge, but everyone carried a little black ruler to measure the gas in the tank. The tank held 10 gallons—enough to propel the car for 225–250 miles.

The Ford was an excellent hill-climber with plenty of power, but it sputtered when it went up a very steep hill. It was starved for gas because the fuel couldn't get to the carburetor. Sometimes the driver had to put the car in reverse and back it up the hill; it had more power in reverse anyway.

The Model T's lubrication system employed a combination of gravity and splash. With no dipstick to check the oil, the driver had to get down on his knees to turn one of the two pet-cocks on the lower half of the flywheel housing. Oil running out of the top of the petcock meant

oil had to be added. Sometimes the Model T used too much oil.

The water circulation was based on the principle that warm water rises and cold water sinks. There was no water pump.

People learned from necessity how to repair their own cars, and they liked to tinker with them. A set of tools came with each Model T. Parts were made by the millions and stocked in warehouses all over the country; they could be found in any small town—or farmer's barn. A muffler cost $2, a front fender was $3, and a front spring would set the owner back $4.

The Model T was the first big vehicle made for the man who couldn't afford a very expensive car. In 1908, consumers bought 59,486 Model T's for $850 each. By 1916, the number sold had risen to 577,036—and the price had fallen to $360.

Ford Motor Co. was established on June 16, 1903, with $150,000 capital. Henry Ford was the president, head of engineering and general manager. There were few stockholders. It was the first large company to produce motorcars

New Model T Fords lined up in a row circa 1914. Photo courtesy Moser Motor Sales.

Henry Ford and Edsel B. Ford with the 15-millionth Ford Quadricycle, May 26, 1927.
From the Collections of Henry Ford Museum & Greenfield Village.

and the first to employ assembly-line production techniques.

When Henry Ford started building cars, he knew the difference between steel and iron, and that was about all. He sent to England for a man who knew how to make steel commercially. He discovered that he had to use a steel alloy made with vanadium to achieve a lighter, stronger material for the Model T. The vanadium-steel, heat-treated springs were mounted so that they were practically part of the frame. As a result, the same strain which sent ordinary springs to the junk pile had no effect on these springs.

The four cylinders in the Model T's 20-horsepower engine were cast in one block integral with water jackets and the upper half of the crankcase. The water-jacketed cylinder head was detachable, permitting access to all parts of the engine—the simplest, surest construction ever embodied in the manufacture of an automobile engine.

When the engine slowed, the lights dimmed and flickered because the electric lighting was secured from the low-tension magneto. The driver found it better to drive in low gear with a fast-turning motor than in a higher gear with the engine revolving slowly.

The magneto or magnet generator furnished with every Model T was built into the power plant. There were no belts, brushes, contact points, moving wires or commutator. It was the simplest magneto built, and was noted for the absence of magneto troubles. Direct-driven by the engine shaft with a rotor a part of the flywheel and the stator a part of the engine, it did its work as long as the engine ran.

The motor, the silent, velvety, planetary transmission, the "new" Ford magneto generator, the cooling system and the oiling system were all made in one compact, enclosed unit.

Henry Ford was the first manufacturer to put in steering on the left-hand side. He realized it was more important that the driver have a good view of the car coming toward him on his left than of the ditch on his right. And it was far better for the ladies, who could exit the vehicle and step directly onto the boardwalk instead of the muddy street. ☆

My First Love Was a Lizzie T

By Robert Longfellow

In 1930 and before the Great Depression reached us, I was 12 years old, living with my parents on a farm. Our property was adjacent to my dad's parents' ranch. They specialized in raising registered Hereford cattle. We lived about 6 miles from the town of Republic, Kan.

My brother Jack and my Uncle Bill were a few years older than I was. This margin of age permitted them to participate in more adult chores, such as driving the Model T Ford stake truck to the fields when the workers required tools and equipment. I pleaded and begged to be part of this action, but they always ended up saying I was too young—and anyway, I didn't know how to drive.

Uncle Bill was an exceptionally gifted person when it came to mechanics. He converted an old, decrepit 1925 Ford coupe into a stripped-down going machine. It consisted of only the barest of equipment—frame, wheels, steering wheel, dashboard, hood and engine. But after a careful tune-up and overhaul, we flew like the wind when we headed her down the old country dirt roads. Strangers looked at us like they didn't believe what they were seeing. We selected "Lizzie T" as her name.

Grasping the steering wheel firmly, I knew that the idea was to keep the wheels on the two long planks that had been secured across the center of the bridge.

The one uncomfortable thing about this contraption was that the only thing between the hard bumps and our bottoms was the round gasoline tank upon which we sat. Nonetheless, we made many trips in her to the Republic River for an afternoon of swimming, fishing or scouting for future action among the bottomland watermelon patches.

By watching Uncle Bill when he prepared to start Lizzie T, I quickly learned how to set the spark and gas lever, then set the brake lever back until it clicked in the slot, and how to twist the two wires under the dash to turn on the switch. Last, but not least, he placed a block or brick in front of a back tire, for Lizzie T was known to sometimes leap forward as much as two feet when she started up. The person doing the cranking knew this too, and without the block, he had to be quick on his feet!

But even with all this accumulated know-how, I was still told I was too young to drive.

Our Grandmother Longfellow was a dear and understanding lady. During bad storms when we kids couldn't be outdoors, she read wonderful stories to us that captured our interest and encouraged constructive thinking. Grandmother Longfellow was a born teacher, and she knew how to motivate youngsters.

I always confessed my problems to her, and frequently emphasized my dismay at being told I wasn't old enough to drive. I guess that after hearing this complaint over and over again, she decided to do something about it.

One afternoon, when all of our people were in the field or busy elsewhere, Grandmother Longfellow called me into the house. "I need you to make a trip to Republic for me," she said. "I need some fabric dye, and you can get it at the hardware store. Do you think you can start Billy's car?"

I leaped to my feet, thrilled to think that she trusted me to make the long trip by myself. We poured a gallon of tractor gas into Lizzie and filled the radiator with water. I found my shoes and straw hat while Grandmother tucked the sample box of dye and two dollar bills into my bib overalls.

As a parting comment, she suggested I avoid the main street and park on a side street to keep out of traffic. She then returned to the house and left me on my own. As I look back, I remember Republic as a town with wooden walks, a wide dirt main street and very few stores. I doubt if there was any traffic, horses or cars, considering the day and time of day.

Lizzie T was parked facing the road to Republic. Uncle Bill had shown me the easy way to start the car by jacking up the rear wheels. I did so, and after setting the levers, I cranked a couple of turns and she immediately kicked off. I jumped behind the steering wheel and noticed that the rear wheels were really spinning. I couldn't get off and remove the jack, so I bodily rocked back and forth until the jack flipped off, and old Lizzie T and I flew out of the driveway in a cloud of dust. I must have made the first turn on two wheels, but I was merrily on my way!

I waved as I passed our neighbors' houses,

hoping my friends would see me and gasp at my ability to drive. However, I did not dare take my eyes off the road, as the front wheels dropped into deep ruts, jerking the steering wheel back and forth.

After a few miles of hanging on for dear life, I saw ahead of me the old, narrow, wooden bridge spanning the rain-swollen Republican River. I adjusted the gas lever for a slower speed and hoped no one else was on the bridge, as this would have meant I had to stop. It was only a one-lane bridge.

Grasping the steering wheel firmly, I knew that the idea was to keep the wheels on the two long planks that had been secured across the center of the bridge. As we slowly crawled across, I could see the churning waters below through the missing boards and big holes under the planks.

But we made it, and I was breathing a little easier when we arrived at the outskirts of Republic. Suddenly realizing that I had left the car jack at home and couldn't use it to get started again, I parked Lizzie T on a steep downhill grade so I could make a coasting start.

The local hardware store had the dye Grandmother Longfellow needed, and I was anxious to get back to Lizzie T. She started right up, and I headed home with no problems. I enjoyed the much-too-quick trip.

When I pulled into the drive, a few members of the family were assembled under the big cottonwood trees in Grandmother's yard. After securing Lizzie T and patting her on her hood, I walked up to the group feeling 10 feet tall, even though my admirers greeted me like a child, hugging me and saying they were relieved I got back in one piece!

When I handed Grandmother Longfellow her dye and the change, she whispered in my ear, "I'm so proud of you, Bob. I knew you could do it." They were two wonderful ladies: my Grandmother Longfellow and Lizzie T. ☆

All Steamed Up!

By Russell Stratton

The Steam Age pretty well sizzled out during the 1920s, but it remained long enough for my generation to be thrilled by glamorous railroad locomotives, excited by rare glimpses of fire trucks with steam-powered pumpers, fascinated by steam shovels and road rollers, and entertained by circus calliopes. For many of us, there was also the gratifying distinction of being transported in automobiles powered by steam.

There was something romantic about steam-driven machines clearly lacking in the power apparatus that has replaced them. Without clouds of smoke or churning white vapors, diesel trains seem stodgy and prosaic; fire-truck pumpers with no trailing plumes of smoke are quite uninspiring; and heavy construction equipment is comparatively "ho-hum" to those who remember the earlier machines that awed and fascinated sidewalk superintendents of those days.

My earliest recognition of steam's majesty came at the age of 4, I guess. In the Boston suburb of West Newton, we lived on a residential road that emptied onto busy Washington Street. On the far side of that thoroughfare (which I was sternly forbidden to cross) was a sunken area with several pairs of train tracks. From the sidewalk at the corner of my street I could see only the tops of trains rushing by, and black, white or gray smoke trails swirling above the speeding rooftops. There was always the hope of a jackpot sighting: the simultaneous passing of two express trains heading in opposite directions.

Viewing the action across the wide highway was a great spectator sport, but for getting places, I was chiefly dependent on Dad's "Steamer," named Stanley.

The Stanley Brothers built their once-famous automobiles in Newton. My dad operated a printing business and was active in civic and political affairs, so he was familiar with the Stanley people and their product. By the time I was 4 years old, he owned his third edition of the elite Stanley Steamer.

We rarely ventured far from home, except for vacation trips to some place like Green Harbor, perhaps 20 or 25 miles away. We usually took a Sunday afternoon drive into the countryside, as Dad nursed mighty yearnings for rural living with plenty of open land for farming. I remember little of our experiences with our early Steamers, but I do have a hazy recall of the time Dad drove too close to the beach sands. That Sunday after-noon excursion ended with a team of husky Dobbins dragging the car to the hard-packed roadway to the accompaniment of wisecracks and unsolicited counsel from the bystanders.

Mom observed that "the Stanley can pass anything along the road but a horse-watering trough." Generating steam required water in the boiler, and this necessitated frequent replenish-ment of the water supply. The most convenient sources of water were the capacious watering troughs, strategically located in every town and village for the convenience of four-footed beasts of burden. Horseless carriages, of course, granted priority to their equine brethren when-ever necessary. On a hot summer day, it was amazing how long it took a thirsty horse to drink his fill and move on, obviously enjoying his brother transport's impatience.

It was an added annoyance that travel in a Stanley required advance preparation by way of

> *Generating steam required water in the boiler, and this necessitated frequent replenishment of the water supply. The most convenient sources of water were the capacious watering troughs.*

igniting the kerosene burner beneath the boiler. (In late models, a pilot flame and gasoline fuel speeded things up a bit.) Pressure had to build in the boiler before the car could move under its own power. Once compression was fully achieved, a Stanley could reach speeds uncalculated, as it was said that the vehicle would disintegrate before attaining a limit.

Behind our home was a small shed with wide doors and barely sufficient space to accommodate the car. One beautiful summer Sunday in 1914, Dad torched the burner in preparation for a pleasure drive. Then, other interests inside the house must have claimed his attention. Shortly, my brother and I were distracted from our play by an explosive popping, followed by the strident hissing of released compression. Churning white steam poured out of the shed through the doors, windows and every vent and crack.

Dad heard the blast and rushed from the house. He dashed into the shed and the rolling mass of fog as we stood by helplessly, paralyzed with fear for his safety. Finally he reappeared, none the worse for wear, having successfully turned off the burner flame. Fortunately, the Stanley had a properly operating safety valve on its boiler, preventing a major explosion.

The billows of white gradually disappeared and things returned to normal, but I suspect that the incident had a bearing on the fact that we didn't keep the car much longer, and never replaced it with another Stanley.

In fact, six or seven years passed before we owned another automobile.

By that time, we were living in a rural home 20 miles from Newton. The new car was gasoline-powered. Of this particular model, it was commonly remarked (unintentionally paraphrasing Mother's quip about the Stanley), "It'll pass anything but a gas pump!"

Despite Dad's frightening experience with the Stanley, he had very fond memories of the ease with which it handled. He never really felt at home behind the wheel of a conventional gasoline-fueled automobile. ✯

The Stanley steam taxis were a few years old at the time this photo was taken. The dates on their New Hampshire plates were 1915 and their plates were of the "for hire" issue. Photo courtesy Robert Pat Farrel.

In the days of steamboats on the nation's great waterways, passengers, mail and freight moved first on deeper draft vessels and then onto "packet" boats. The steamer Joe Fowler (right) operated from 1881 to 1912 and ran from Paducah, Ky., to Evansville, Ind., making the round trip in 25 hours. This painting is part of the flood-wall murals at Paducah painted by Robert Dafford.

Those Old Steamboat Days

By Henry S. Wood

*I*n the early part of the last century, when I was 10 to 12 years of age, the steamboat packets of the western rivers were still in their heyday. My uncle, Albert Wood, was a clerk on one of these packets that ran between Louisville and Cincinnati on the Ohio River, and this gave me the privilege of making several trips up and down the river.

I'll never forget one trip I made down the river from Vevey, Ind., to Louisville on the steamer Queen City.

The Queen City was one of the most picturesque and ornate stern-wheelers on the Ohio. She had been built especially for the aristocratic trade between Pittsburgh and Cincinnati, but in her later years, she was sometimes used between Cincinnati and Louisville when the river was low.

On this August day, the boat's pilot, Capt. Jesse Hughes, was kind enough to allow me to ride with him in the pilothouse, even though it was against the rules of steamboat navigation. At that time, it was the height of my ambition to become a steamboat pilot.

There were landings every few miles along the river, and the local packet would seesaw back and forth

The deckhands, or "rousters," as they were called, could rest between landings. They worked a full day for $1 and their meals. They slept in quarters in the hull of the boat.

across the river from one landing to another, picking up passengers and what freight there was. At one landing there might be a drove of hogs, at another a veal calf or a crate of chickens or a case of eggs. When the boat landed, the second clerk, or "mud clerk," as he was called, would rush out on the stage plank, and as soon as it hit the bank, he would usher the passengers aboard. Then the deckhands—the "rousters"—would carry on the freight.

When the passengers and freight were loaded, the chief mate would pull a rope, giving the bell on top of the boat a loud gong. This signaled the pilot that the boat was ready to leave. The pilot had a number of ropes running from the pilothouse on top of the boat to bells in the engine room on the lower deck. One bell told the engineer to back up, while other bells signaled the engineer to go ahead. They could also use these bells to signal the speed they wanted.

The pilot would blow the boat whistle at the approach of a landing, and if there were passengers or freight to go, they would signal the boat by waving a handkerchief during daylight or a swinging lantern at night.

On this August morning, we had just gone a few miles down the river when Capt. Hughes noticed a man on the Indiana side at the mouth of a creek, waving his handkerchief. After we landed, I discovered that this man lived in a shanty boat tied to the bank in the mouth of the creek. He had a couple of large sacks and a number of bundles of bark. I lost interest in the pilothouse for the moment and turned my attention to the man and his cargo.

His name was Wilson Crist, and he made his living fishing, and gathering roots and herbs. He was taking his shipment to Madison, Ind., where there was one of the largest buyers of medicinal roots and herbs in the Midwest.

This interested me very much, for I lived with my parents in a wooded section of Kentucky, and I figured that if I learned about some of the wild roots and herbs, I could make some spending money by gathering them.

Mr. Crist took a small sack from his large bag and showed me some valuable ginseng roots. From another sack he showed me the less valuable roots, such as yellow root, mayapple root, a couple of kinds of snakeroot and some wild ginger. The bark in the bundles had been peeled from young elm trees, called slippery elm, and was widely used by manufacturers of medicine.

When he left the boat at Madison, I could turn my interest back to the pilothouse. The next landing down the river was made at the bottom of a steep cliff called Plow Handle Point. There was a crude shanty up on the steep hillside, and it was only accessible by boat.

This shanty was the home of a notorious character along the river called "Ma Gaylord." The pilot told me her story. She was a squatter and did not own the ground upon which her shanty was built. But the hill was so steep and rugged that no one ever disturbed her.

A vagabond would come down the river and

Ma Gaylord would take him in. She would first teach him the art of fishing for catfish with a trotline. Then, when she was sure that he was not a revenue officer in disguise, she would take him up the steep cliff and teach him the more skilled art of making moonshine whiskey.

When the boat landed, a dark-skinned young man got on board with a tub of catfish. He sold some of them to the head cook on the boat and the rest were iced down and taken to Louisville, where they were sold. I talked with him and he told me he was half-Indian. Later I wished I had gotten to know him better. When I grew to manhood and became a feature writer, I tried a number of times to get a story about the river life of Ma Gaylord, but was told by everyone that her isolated cliff was off-limits to strangers.

The next stop the boat made was at Dean's Landing. Here the Dean family, who lived back on the hill on the Indiana side of the river, had 2,000 acres planted in peach orchards. The boat was loaded nearly full with bushel baskets of peaches.

When the passengers and freight were loaded, the chief mate would pull a rope, giving the bell on top of the boat a loud gong. This signaled the pilot that the boat was ready to leave.

All the rousters on the boat were put to work. John DuRand, the head mate, known all along the river for his flow of strong invective in driving rousters, must have been at his best. I never had heard such a flow of profanity; however, the boat was soon loaded and we were on our way again.

The only other exciting event took place at Oldham Landing, halfway between Madison and Louisville. Here, an unruly bull that seemed to object to going to market gave the rousters a hard time.

The Queen City no longer exists. Many of the good boats on the Ohio were destroyed during the famous ice flow of 1918. Most of the landings along the river are grown up in weeds. However, I'll never forget my rides with the kind pilot, Jesse Hughes. No longer do we find shanty boatmen like Wilson Crist, with his medicinal roots. But I have never been able to live as much in 24 hours as I did on that August day back in the early days of the 20th century. ✯

Indiana's First Aeroplane Pilot

By Adm. Raymond H. Beyer

One morning back in 1911, we heard a noise outside, something strange we had never heard before. Running outside, we saw an aeroplane flying over our house in South Bend, Ind. When we waved at the man who was sitting in front of the wings, he waved back.

Reading the paper that night, we learned that the pilot was Calbraith P. Rogers, who was making the first coast-to-coast flight. Later we learned that he had left New York on Sept. 19, 1911. It took him 49 days to make the trip, although he actually spent only 82 hours and 4 minutes in the air. He stopped 69 times—including 19 crash landings—before he completed the 3,220-mile trek. When he finally landed in Pasadena, Calif., on Nov. 5, he had one leg in a cast, and only a rudder and single wing strut remained from his original Wright Pusher aeroplane.

But from the moment I saw that aeroplane, I was addicted to flying. I spent my entire life in aeronautics.

My Uncle Bill, head machinist at Studebaker's, and his two friends, Joe, a blacksmith, and Art, a cabinetmaker, also became interested in aeroplanes. They decided to build and fly one. Two years later,

The author, Raymond H. Beyer, in the cockpit, 1919.

it was ready to take to the air.

"Come on and get going!" Bill yelled at me as he pushed me down into the cockpit and snapped the buckle on the seat belt. The seat was too big for me; I could barely touch the rudder bar with the tips of my shoes. Bill's homemade motor churned the propeller that Joe had hand-whittled. Art and Joe hung onto the wings, struggling desperately to keep the Blériot monoplane from racing down the field before I was ready.

"OK! Let's see if you can fly this thing!" Bill shouted as he scurried away. Suddenly, the notion of taking that homemade aeroplane up into the heavens above South Bend on that August day in 1913 frightened the wits out of me. At 10 years old, I knew I was too young to be hobnobbing with angels; what would St. Peter think? What would my folks think when they found out? Squinting, I banished all such thoughts out of my mind. I shoved the throttle forward, flipping Joe and Art, my human brakes, flat on their faces.

Earlier that morning, while chickens still huddled on their roosts, Mr. Blériot's model of a channel-floating aeroplane had been rolled out of Joe's blacksmith shop. Its wings were made from the best maple Art could find, and were covered with linen of the highest quality, purchased at Robertson's department store. Bill's hand-coddled motor sat in the fuselage with all the pride of Queen Mary on her throne. The glimmer from the lanterns made the holding wires flicker like beads of ice draped around a lady's neck. The fellows who followed the horses pulling the plane through the dark streets bubbled with excitement!

The only exceptions to this mirthful gaiety were Bill and I. Bill was filled with red-eye, and I was loaded with disappointment. During the preceding year while the craft was being built, I had begged, pleaded and bawled to fly the crate. No mention had been made to my folks; they had no enthusiasm for the notion of their only son cloud-hopping. But I suffered visions of the plane crumpled up in some junkyard, flown and spent, and me still stuck on the ground. As they pulled the plane through the darkness, the horses' hooves beat out a thumping taunt meant just for me: "No, you can't fly it … no, you can't fly it."

Suddenly Bill grabbed the reins from Art's callused hands and yelled, "Whoa there! Whoa!"

"Listen, you guys," he declared, "with two bottles and one drink, I still haven't got enough guts to fly this hunk of junk!" Then, knees buckling, he flopped face-first in the dirt. Art and Joe looked at each other sheepishly.

Suddenly I viewed the three with renewed hope. Bill had had too much to drink, Art had only one leg, and Joe was just too fat to fit in the seat. "Come on, Bill, please let me fly it!" I begged. "We're not going to quit *now*, are we?"

After a long squabble, they came to a decision. "OK, you can fly it," Bill slurred. "But remember one thing: If you have to wreck it, smash it up easy, 'cause your folks will be right smart mad at me if I have to bring you home in a basket." Reluctantly, Bill staggered over to one side and started waving his long arms. Then he yelled, "Come on kid, let's kiss the angels!"

So *that's* how I found myself in my present predicament.

The fingers on my left hand tightened on the elevator wheel like a drowning man clutching at a straw while my right hand froze onto the throttle. My nerves were vibrating like banjo strings at a square dance. Dirt and dust filled my eyes, and my mouth was as dry as Bill's last bottle. Too scared to start and too brave to quit, I pushed the throttle wide open and went high-tailing across the pasture in a cloud of dust.

The machine bucked and fluttered all over Mussel's field, so I had to work the rudder bar faster than Casey Jones at the throttle. A fence at the far end of the field approached faster than the 20th Century screaming through the freight yard. Trees loomed before me, and suddenly that fence seemed as tall as the town water tower!

When I pushed the elevator wheel forward, the tail leaped off the ground, bouncing us along on Art's old bicycle wheels. The seat of my pants cracked against the seat, reminding me of the razor strap my dad sometimes applied to the same spot. That fence was growing taller and faster than Jack's beanstalk! Too scared to think, I yanked the wheel back into my belly, jumping the fence and blasting the top rail into smithereens.

Lincoln Beachy had said, in one of his letters to Bill, "When … you are on your first flight, proceed in a straight line until you conquer the controls." And fly in a straight line I did—but the line was crowded with trees, houses and barns thicker than farmers at a county fair! One big old oak tree insisted on standing directly in my line of flight; consequently, it had to sacrifice two of its upper limbs. At that moment, an acorn of a boy matured to the brink of manhood.

I had never gone faster or farther than a horse could trot in one day so I had no conception of miles. The vast expanse scared the day-lights out of me. I was lost! The earth below looked strange—roads, creeks and rivers crept everywhere, marked only by glaring sunlight. Pushing the rudder bar, I leaned in the same direction, the shoulder harness hugging me tighter than a bear protecting her cubs. The aeroplane gave me a hobbyhorse ride, making my head dance with sickening dizziness.

When my eyes cleared, the sun was above me once more, but I knew nothing of where I was going. My stomach was as empty as King Tut's tomb, for my breakfast and I had parted company somewhere during that last spin. The only direction I was sure of was down, and I was too far down already. I heard the trees whisper "Hello" as they stretched their limbs to welcome me in a dangerous embrace.

I flew straight, in circles, up and down, gliding like a roller coaster, all the time quivering like jelly. On the ground, if you're lost, you simply asked a farmer for directions; up here, there was no one to ask. To be lost in the blue sky is really befuddling; all directions look the same, especially when the sun is perched at 12 o'clock high, for there are no shadows. All I could see were roads fanning out like a giant cobweb.

Mussel's field was somewhere below, but as far as I knew, I could have been over Canada. From the air, one section of land looked just like the next. My heart in my throat, I managed to gently pull back on the elevator wheel, making for the blue above.

In his letters, Mr. Beachy had never mentioned air bumps on hot days, but I soon discovered them. The bottom fell rapidly out of the seat, flattening my stomach against the seat belt. In vain I yanked and slammed the wheel, and we fell down … down … then instantly soared straight up, forcing my small frame against the seat. We bobbed up and down like a buggy on a washboard road.

Then, abruptly, the bumps ceased—and I found myself *flying* in a wonderfully silent and serene world. The view was breathtaking, and I forgot all about being lost. I was viewing an absolutely marvelous sight known only to God's winged creatures.

Now I saw that the earth was laid out in squares, with each section bearing a shading of its own. Little tufts of cotton floated through the beguiling blue, their dark bases supporting snowy crowns. Migrating seagulls glided along with me, seemingly nodding their welcome greeting.

Now, slowly, I leaned toward the left wing, tipping into an easy turn, and then the earth came to a sudden end, dipping into a mass of bluish-white frothy streaks. Again I was chewing on my heart, for I realized I was skirting the shore of Lake Michigan. I had been to its beach just once, and the trip had taken all day by horse and buggy. I was a long way from home and my landing field. My knowledge of geography was limited, but simple logic told me to reverse my course. And just then, I spied a railroad track slithering in that direction.

Hugging that set of rails tighter than a puppy in a thunderstorm, I glimpsed a glitter on the distant horizon, and knew it had to be the golden dome at the University of Notre Dame. Banking left, I sailed straight for that lovely pot of gold. A big birthday cake had never looked more inviting! Circling wide, I crossed the St. Joseph River and headed for Mussel's field.

My eyes opened wide with astonishment, for the field was surrounded by buggies and curious onlookers. As I circled the pasture, my landing spot seemed smaller than a tugboat on the ocean. Mr. Beachy had written, "Cut the motor and glide into the wind for a landing." As easy as spreading jelly on a biscuit—but what would happen if the jelly slid into your lap? Clipping rails off the fence would surely splatter me!

The wind, blowing strongly in all directions, instilled too much fear in me to cut the motor. Trying to collect the guts to land, I circled the field again, glancing at the crowd below who were flailing their arms, imploring me to land.

Twice I headed for the field and pulled back up; that mile-high fence terrified me. On the next turn, however, the motor suddenly coughed and sputtered. The horsepower was gone with the wind, and we slipped into a fast descent, rocketing toward the dear old sod.

It took all the power a small boy could muster to pull that wheel back. Miraculously, the fence slipped under us; even so, I thought I could feel its splinters jabbing the seat of my knickers. Those bicycle wheels smacked the ground harder than Joe could whack a red-hot horseshoe, bouncing us back into the air. As the crate leaped and lurched across Mussel's cow pasture like a bucking bronco, the flimsy, wire-spoked wheels finally gave up the ghost and buckled. I learned firsthand that timeless truth: "The hardest thing in flying is the ground."

Across the field, a mass of hysterical humanity surged toward me, shouting and waving their arms. I looked again. Sure enough, Bill—now sober—was leading the mob. My preposterous wings and I were still intact—except for the landing gear, a propeller and one morning meal. No longer was I just scared—merely petrified, for I knew the experience that I'd managed to survive was immaterial compared to the reception I'd receive from my folks at home.

"Boy, are we proud of you!" Bill screeched as he reached my side and dragged me out of the wreck. "Did you know, feller, you're the first one to ever fly an aeroplane in Indiana?" ★

Flying High

By Naomi Bradfield

"How would you like to fly in a real airplane?" Father asked me.

Would I? I was about 10 at the time, and back then the mere sound of an airplane brought folks out in a hurry, looking skyward. There was not a kid in the neighborhood who would turn down a chance to be up in a plane. Naturally I said, "Yes," and that very evening my folks took me out to the airport in Lansing, Mich., where we lived.

The field was crowded, and a thick rope separated us from the lone plane that was warming up. It was a little beauty of a cabin cruiser, and a young man in flying gear stood by its side. Floodlights lit the area, starkly outlining plane and pilot in bold relief.

At last the rope was taken down, and before I knew it, I was one of the small group that was headed for the plane. I knew it cost money; later, I learned that the price was $5 for about 10 minutes of flight.

Eagerly, yet half afraid, I boarded the plane and found myself being pushed to the side. At the same time, the young pilot cleared the steps with a bound, slamming the door after him. For a brief instant he looked at me, then smiled and slid into his seat.

"You can stand right behind my seat," he said. I thanked him.

The roar of the plane taking off startled me. I was, and still am, hard of hearing. I was also starting to feel nervous and I wondered if this idea of flying was such a good one after all.

The takeoff was so smoothly accomplished that it was a moment or two before I realized that we were off the ground, and climbing higher and higher. I gripped the back of the pilot's seat firmly, expecting to slide all the way back to the tail of the plane. All I could

hear was a loud buzz like a million bees. Then the sound settled down to a steady hum as the pilot leveled the plane off.

"Everybody all right?" he shouted. The response was enthusiastic, even though my own voice was rather weak.

It was not long before I began to enjoy myself. Looking down, I saw the beautiful lights of the city below. I could not help drawing in my breath. As the plane circled slowly, it was like watching a pinwheel, but much more lovely.

We went higher. Suddenly I felt a pain in my left ear, then another in my right as a loud pop! exploded in my head. "Oh, my ears!" I cried. The pilot handed me something over his shoulder.

"Here, chew this stick of gum. It will take the funny feeling away from your ears," he said.

I took the gum and almost dropped it. I found out he was right, but more than that …

"I can hear!" I shouted. "I can hear everything!" I yelled, jumping up and down. "I'm almost deaf, but I can hear!"

Everyone laughed and the pilot smiled. I will never forget his voice. "Fine. Well, it's time to go down now, folks. Here we go."

I was sad to have to leave, and for some reason the eyes of the pilot lingered on mine as I said my goodbye and thank-you. I ran to my parents and told them excitedly that I could hear.

My joy lasted only 24 hours before I was again back in that dull land of guesswork and reading lips. Somehow, I never felt too bad about it, for the airplane trip had been worth every penny my dad spent. Then again, the imprint of that young pilot's face has always been fresh in my mind. It was a kind face, and it was years before I knew who it was that I had met— Howard Hughes. ✫

Wooden Cars & Iron Men

By Ray Young

About the time that steam was forcing the sailing ship off the high seas, it was creating another breed of giants on the high iron. If ever a group could be called "men of steel," it was those men most closely connected with the early days of the iron horse. Some of railroading's rugged pioneer beginnings lasted on until World War I.

To the modern American, early railroading suggests balloon smokestacks, giant headlights with hand-painted scenes of Niagara Falls, and maybe a buffalo herd stopping a train. To those on the spot, however, the time recalls the torrent of sweat that carried coal to the firebox, or the race across an icy boxcar's top in the dark when the engineer whistled "Down brakes!"

The engineer and fireman had the more romantic jobs on the snorting, smoking locomotive. The engineer's task was easier, but carried more responsibility. In the early days especially, he was the man who kept the train from plowing into the rear of another, or the head end of one he met on a single-track line. The fireman could jump, but he would have been glad to change his backaches for the engineer's headaches.

In the days of the steamer—which carried through World War II—the fireman lived for the day when someone ahead of him would die or retire, or the road would expand, and he could move over to the right-hand side of the cab. Meanwhile, the traditional tool of his trade was a large coal scoop. With this shovel and a large iron bar for breaking up clinkers, he had to keep enough fuel going into the hungry furnace mouth to permit the engine to haul its 25 or 30 freight cars over the tougher grades on the line.

On runs with short trains or local hauls, this was not too bad a job. In heavy freight service, or on a line with many hills, the fireman earned every cent he got. The job entailed more than merely throwing coal. He had to keep a steady and even cover over the grates without cutting off the flame, to get the best combustion. When not sweating at this, he spent his free time cracking large chunks of coal into manageable bits, checking steam pressure and water level, and keeping constant watch on his side of the train (where the engineer couldn't see). He also sometimes spelled the engineer at the throttle, in an early form of on-the-job training.

The fireman's lot often depended on how well he and the engineer got along. A good fireman-engineer team meant that the man at the throttle used his steam to best advantage and got the best downhill start to make the next grade. A poor engineer, or one with a grudge, could waste steam and change a routine firing job into a frantic, sweat-soaked workout. Of course, if the fireman couldn't keep up, the engine's performance suffered, so this worked both ways. By the 1920s, the larger freight engines were coming equipped with automatic stokers, but the older, smaller "teakettles" relied on muscle power as the ultimate source of their steam.

The toughest men, however, were the brakemen. There were at least three on an average 25-car freight, although there could be more, depending on the length of the train and the number of hills.

The head brakeman rode in the locomotive and was responsible for the first group of cars. The brakemen, like the locomotive's crew, were under command of the conductor (himself an ex-brakeman), who rode in the comfort of the caboose. For the most part, the old-school brakemen had sole responsibility for seeing that brakes were set and released on command.

The "parlor brakeman" got his name from his station at the end of the train, where he rode in the caboose. This term showed some ironic humor, because he might not see much of the inside of the "shanty." If the train made an unscheduled stop, he was the one to walk back with a flag, lantern or flares to alert any following trains, and then run back to the train when the whistle blew. He did a lot of running.

The toughest job, however, went to the "swing brakeman" in the middle of the train. He (or they, if the train was exceptionally long or running in the hills), rode where there was no heat and no shelter—atop the cars. With luck, he might have a gondola or flatcar to ride on, with something to lessen the force of the wind. In the 1880s, before air brakes were perfected, the swing brakeman was often pictured standing atop a boxcar, gazing out into the glorious dawn or sunset, enjoying the summer breeze. This, like many other contemporary views of the working man, was a bit idealized. The railroads didn't pay brakemen to just ride. Their job was to set and release brakes in a snowstorm or freezing rain, and live to tell about it.

Riding atop the train, the brakeman carried a short, thick club. To save time, he often waited at the end of a boxcar having the brake wheel, which resembled a car's steering wheel on an upright post. At the signal, he thrust the stick between the spokes of the wheel and used it as a lever to turn the wheel and thus force the brakes against the car wheels. Then he jumped across the gap to the next car, ran down the shaking, swaying roof, and did the same thing there.

In warm weather this wasn't too bad, and even brief summer showers were tolerable; in fact, they could offer a welcome opportunity to cool off. But when the snow piled up on the narrow boardwalks atop the cars, or rain froze there, it was different. The brakeman had to make his way half by instinct and half by feel from one brake wheel to the next. And every few feet there lay a chasm, which although only about a dozen feet deep, had at its bottom the grinding car wheels. A good brakeman had to be a virtual cat, both in footing and night vision.

The trouble with the old hand brakes was that they didn't all go on at the same time. This meant that the brakeman had to make sure that those he set would hold long enough for him to set the rest. Often the brakeman would be half-done when the signal to release brakes would send him flying back the way he'd come. Since engineers tended to have the same run for long

periods, they could judge when it was necessary to brake, but weather, stray cows or a late train ahead made it impossible to count on anything.

Yet many brakemen liked the work. On local runs, with frequent coupling or uncoupling of cars, there was a break in the monotony and scurry. The outdoor life and fresh air compensated for the long, chilly winters if a brakeman had a fairly easy route.

For years after the adoption of air brakes and automatic couplers, a good way to spot a former brakeman was by his missing fingers. Until the latter part of the 19th century, cars were coupled with the link-and-pin method. Each car had, at each end, a long rod with its end bent into a circle. Two such rods were held together by a heavy iron pin. The brakeman had to reach between the cars and drop or pull the pin. Often the train would jerk while the brakeman had a finger between link and pin, with the expected results.

The brakeman's stick wasn't always a peaceful instrument, and he had to carry it on some roads in self-defense, long after the air brake became standard in the 1890s. The traveling bum might have left his mark on folk history and popular music, but he wasn't always a happy-go-lucky wayfarer. Many were vicious, and the brakeman was the first to know this. The railroads objected to carrying bums or hoboes, one reason being their tendency to steal anything not nailed down—and that included the contents of sealed freight cars.

The struggle between railroad police and brakemen against the bum was long and bitter. In a roughshod age, the brakeman was expected to keep the train clear of nonpaying passengers, and woe betide the trainman caught winking at their presence. But an experienced or desperate bum was nobody to trifle with, and the brakeman often swung his club to avoid another club or knife.

On the other hand, the bum, tramp or hobo (the name depending on whether he was a loafer, sometime worker, or itinerant laborer headed for a new job) had to cope not only with the elements, but an unsympathetic railroad. The custom of "hopping a freight" arose from necessity.

This enabled the 'bo to board after the train crew had checked the cars and were busy with their own jobs. The astute 'bo would find an open boxcar and crawl in. If the train was

The Royal Hudson, with its wooden cars and iron men, served British Columbia early in the 20th century.

moving, he walked or ran along the track, and then, synchronizing his gait with the train's motion, grabbed a ladder and swung aboard. He then climbed to the top, if on a boxcar, and made his way along the top of the train to a convenient gondola, flatcar or coal car.

Otherwise, he went to a boxcar whose side door was opened (something he determined before hopping aboard) and then swung down inside. This was dangerous, but it had its advantages. It meant that pursuit was unlikely. The brakeman who came down after him couldn't get back out until the train stopped, so the 'bo had a safe place until flushed out at the next stop.

For a harmless individual who hopped a freight merely because he had no money (something commonly done up to the mid-1930s) the train crews seemed unduly strict, to say the least. But for their part, they had seen some of the less harmless elements, and most were hard-bitten enough to take no chances as philanthropists.

Coal cars and other open-top types were good places after the air brake came into use, since there were now few brakemen on the top of the train. "Riding the rods" was not simply a synonym for stealing a free ride. The term arose from some foolhardy souls discovering that the tie rods beneath the cars were ideal for anyone who didn't want to be seen from the train, and thus lessened his chances of being kicked off.

The tie rods were thick, round affairs resembling water pipes. They came down at an angle from the ends of the car and flattened out over most of its length. At each end, rods slanted down to meet others that ran level and parallel below the car's floor. The latter were a comfortable distance below the car's bottom, offering ample space for a body. The 'bo wishing to ride the rods got a wide board. If he had the time and some rope, he fastened it to the rods. If not, he placed it across them, lay on it, and hoped for the best.

Aside from being an uncomfortable perch, this method required considerable nerve or lack of sense. The 'bo had to forget about the ties only a few inches below him and the wheels a few feet away and what they could do if his board slipped. Once the train started, there was no getting off. More than a few such riders

ended up in pieces. This made it preferable to take one's chances with the train crew or occasional "bulls."

Modern car design abolished the tie rods, but many ancient cars continued in use up to the end of World War II. Freight cars have always carried their date or year of manufacture, and around 1945, it was still common to find relics with such notices as "Built 5-90" or "BLT 7-01." They, like their successors for many years, were prone to "hot boxes" caused by the oil-soaked cotton waste that lubricated the wheel bearings catching fire. Until roller bearings became standard after the 1940s, one old-time job remained: The brakeman had to walk along the side of the train and check every wheel "journal box" before starting out—in fair weather or foul. Even so, it wasn't uncommon for a train crew to see someone at the side of the line signaling a "hot box" (holding fingers to nose), and having to stop to put out the fire and let the wheel cool.

With time, the more rugged aspects disappeared. The air brake meant that extra brakemen were a reserve rather than a prime braking force. Old-timers shed few tears when they could ride in the caboose or locomotive for the whole trip. The automatic coupler saved hands and toes. As the age of steam neared its end, the automatic stoker or change to fuel oil on the bigger engines meant that the fireman became more of a technician and less of a laborer.

Many old-time railroad men tended to glamorize the day of the fire shovel and brakeman's club after steel cars replaced the old wooden ones. But while the muscular fireman, glistening in the red light of the furnace, makes a stirring picture, the one who posed for it often thought differently at the time, and while railway travel and equipment changed greatly, human nature evidently did not.

The engineer who fired a drag freight by hand on a mountain run might sneer at the diesel fireman in the 1940s. That same steam engineer might well have started under an engineer from an even older school, who told him in 1910: "Boy, you don't know how easy you have it or what work is. I started out firin' wood, and gettin' my hands as full o' splinters as a ... ." ☆

I Was a Harvey Girl

By Marie Lundgren

Editor's Note: The Harvey Co. operated a lunch and dining room in St. Louis' Union Station beginning in 1914. Union Station has now been revitalized, including a rehabilitated Harvey House lunchroom and three theaters. —K.T.

During the 1940s and 1950s, Union Station in St. Louis was an ex-citing place to work—and we Harvey Girls had fun jobs.

Fred Harvey founded the Fred Harvey Co. in the mid-19th century. For nearly a century the company brought good food at reasonable prices in clean, elegant restaurants to the traveling public.

When I worked for the company—known simply as "Fred Harvey"—it was owned by Fred Harvey's three sons. Harvey Houses consisted of attractive hotels, restaurants and gift shops that stretched from Wisconsin Dells, Chicago, St. Louis and Kansas City to California, catering to travelers by rail.

Fred Harvey also operated smaller dining rooms along the routes for stopover meals. Santa Fe, the plushest line of them all, offered the ultimate in Harvey dining-car service, complete with waiters in white coats, a vase with a fresh rose on each linen-covered table, crystal glasses and beautiful place settings. Food served on the varying menus was the very finest, and Fred Harvey coffee became so popular that it was eventually sold in gift shops all along the line.

Santa Fe's three elegant trains, the Chief, Super Chief and El Capitan, were comfortable and exciting. El Capitan offered the last word in luxury, with high-level domed cars and luggage stored in compartments below the coaches, easily accessible if necessary.

I worked in the newsstand in the center of the midway at Union Station, directly opposite the 28 tracks, where trains moved in and out all day and most of the night. At times the midway was so jammed with travelers that I literally had to battle my way to the stand.

The Yellow Cab concourse was close by the newsstand, and the Red Cap Circle a bit farther on, past the stationmaster's office. The ticket office at the other end of the station was a beehive of activity. The passenger agents always had the funniest stories of their encounters with the travelers.

President Harry Truman often arrived at Union Station on his way home to Independence, Mo., when headed back to the nation's capital. He would shake hands with us and say, "My Harvey Girls! Hello there!" and we felt that we were special to him. He often came through after he was no longer president, too, and he was the same lively person. Between trains, he'd perch on a corner of the desk in the stationmaster's office and chat with anyone who cared to stop.

We saw Tallulah Bankhead berate her maid, and we saw Red Skelton a bit the worse for a stop at the bar in his drinking days. But most of the notables were quiet and unassuming. We were a bit subdued at the arrival of criminals in handcuffs, surrounded by guards; some tried to hide their faces, while others acted very nonchalant.

All manner of people passed through Union Station, from the very wealthy to the ragged beggar trying to avoid the railroad detectives as he slipped in out of the snow or rain.

Our Harvey House was well patronized by residents of the city, and Sundays found the station crowded with diners from St. Louis and East St. Louis, across the river in Illinois.

Union Station was built in the late 1800s and was the world's largest train shed, modeled after the medieval walls of Carcassonne, France, by the architect Theodore Link.

The soaring tower held the traffic controller's room and was accessible by elevator. The clock in the tower always gave St. Louis downtowners the correct time—railroad time.

I was proud to be a Harvey Girl! ⭐

Both trolley and horse-drawn carriage had their place in the quaint lore of moving about in cities back in the Good Old Days.

Trolleys of the 1920s

By Allen W. Cooper

Around 1920, most large cities had a well-developed system of electric cars, following the horse-drawn trolleys of late 19th century. These systems developed on nickel fares until they were the hub around which most of the city's business revolved. Without streetcars, one either walked, or rode a bicycle or horse. There was a great need for a convenient and inexpensive way to get around, and streetcars were the answer.

The electric car system in the twin cities of Minneapolis-St. Paul was rated second only to the Los Angeles system in efficiency and service to the public. The Twin City Lines had over 500 miles of track and around 700 cars in daily use. They had three car stations (or barns) in Minneapolis, and two in St. Paul, and a smaller one in Stillwater. There were also business offices and shops in St. Paul.

Without streetcars, one either walked, or rode a bicycle or horse. There was a great need for a convenient and inexpensive way to get around, and streetcars were the answer.

A network of car lines in each city served most neighborhoods, and there were inter-urban lines running to Minnetonka and other lake areas, such as Excelsior. In St. Paul, a single-track line led to Stillwater, 20 miles away on the St. Croix River. It had feeder lines from Wildwood Park to White Bear and Mahtomedi.

This empire of tracks and equipment served the people well until the general use of autos cut down their revenues. By the 1950s, all the tracks had been taken up and the cars disposed of. The decline set in about 1921, when fares were raised from 5 to 6 cents. But for two fares, one could ride the breadth of both cities—a transportation bargain!

The late-model standard trolley car of the Twin City Lines seated 50 people. But in rush-hour traffic, it often carried well over 100, with the aisle packed and many riding on the rear platform. Such a car weighed over 46,000 pounds, or 23 tons. It had air brakes and was powered by four 60-hp electric motors, one geared to each of four trucks in a ratio of about three revolutions of a motor to one of the wheels. Power was generated at St. Anthony Falls and carried by high-voltage lines to smaller transformer stations where it was changed to 600 volts, direct current.

In 1922 I became a motorman for the Twin City Lines. I continued this work until the middle of 1925. Upon being assigned to the East Seventh Street car station as a student, I was paid 20 cents per hour until I had spent 180 hours under the supervision of regular line motormen.

In 1922, new motormen and conductors were paid 48 cents an hour, 50 cents in their second year and 51 cents thereafter. Years later, upon union-ization of the employees, the scale went to $1.10. We furnished our own uniforms. Those of us who were single took meals at the Trolley Café just across the street from the car station. Meals there ran from 40–60 cents, with breakfast as low as 30 cents.

Half-a-hundred motormen ate at the Trolley Café, along with others from nearby factories. The place was busy most of the day and far into the night. Either the electric player piano or the jukebox was usually going. Dropping a nickel into its slot brought the piano to life, but quite a few brass slugs from pre-Volstead days found their way into the slot, too—along with more than a few washers. Someone finally discovered that a penny worked as well as a nickel, and from that time on, the piano played more often. One day a man came from the piano-leasing company, and along with the restaurant owner, opened the coin box to divide the money. When they saw all those pennies, their faces dropped. Soon afterward the piano disappeared.

In the Loop area, the motorman operated the trolley track switches electrically from a distance of 50–60 feet. When these switches were thrown, they snapped with a report like a pistol's. After rain, the water ran along in the groove and into the switch. When the switch was activated, water was thrown 8–10 feet into the air. In spring, when snow was melting, the groove was full of ice water. One motorman told of seeing two frisky young ladies, carrying purses and bags, crossing the street near the switch. The temptation was too great, and he threw the switch just as the ladies stepped over the rails. The girls "dropped their bags and parcels, threw their arms into the air, and screamed at the top of their voices," he reported. They should have sued the company.

Sometimes in winter, the copper trolley wires broke due to the cold. The crew who discovered the break picked up the wire with insulated clamps and tied the wires together from the roof of a car. Later a wire car came and repaired the break. When I first saw such a break, it puzzled me why they let the car coast past the break, and the conductor pulled the trolley down and replaced it on the wire beyond the break. There seemed to be power on each side of the broken wires. It was, I discovered, because feeder cables mounted on the poles alongside the tracks supplied current at intervals through the cross wires supporting the main trolley wire.

My favorite of all the cars was the Interurban that ran 20 miles to Stillwater. These cars were heavier and more powerful than local cars and carried 90 pounds of air-brake pressure instead of 75. The line operated cars in both directions on a single track supervised by a dispatcher. The Interurban could climb a hill with an 8-degree grade as easily with 100 passengers as it could when it was empty.

Today, people in many areas would welcome the return of good streetcar service. These cars carried more people farther for less money than any other system yet devised, and they did it with no air pollution and with a high degree of passenger safety and comfort. ☆

This photograph of a streetcar of the 1920s was taken at the Minneapolis car station.

Informing a Nation

Chapter Four

✦✦✦✦✦

"*H*ey, mister, ya wanna buy a paper?"

"Yes'm—just a nickel."

If only I had a nickel for every time I said those lines, I would probably be a rich man today.

You see, I was one of the millions of boys and girls who realized their dream of financial independence back in the Good Old Days by hawking newspapers on the streets of our nation's towns and cities. Well … maybe it wasn't independence, but it put enough jingle in my pocket to take me to the cinema every Saturday afternoon when Mama and Daddy couldn't afford to do it.

And, whether I knew it or not, it started me on a path that would inexorably change my life. From newsboy to printer's "devil" to Linotype operator to reporter to small-town editor I learned the business of informing a nation in the days when a newsman still got ink under his nails—if not in his veins.

Back then life could be as tough as guarding your "territory"—the paperboy's most lucrative street corners in town. In a world often turned upside down by depression, drought and war, one way we kept our sanity was by becoming the best-informed country in the world.

This chapter is dedicated to those who were dedicated to us—and to informing a nation.

—*Ken Tate*

Jim Daly
©
1987

The Kansas Optimist

By Aileen Mallory

Thursday was special when I was growing up. Thursday was press day, the most exciting day of the week at *The Kansas Optimist.* The other kids might hang around the schoolyard or stop at a friend's on the way home. Not me. When 4 o'clock came, I headed for my father's printing office.

Our weekly newspaper was *The Kansas Optimist*; it was a good name for anything of my dad's, although it was already named that when he bought it. Dad was an optimist. He had an inherent faith in the Lord, in mankind in general and in his hometown in particular, and he believed everything would turn out all right eventually. And it usually did, one way or another.

Our family life pretty much revolved around the newspaper. Mother was indoctrinated early. For their honeymoon, Dad took her to see the state printing plant in Topeka! He thought she would be as thrilled with it as he was.

Vacation trips were planned so we could be back by press day. Obviously this tended to limit the length of the trip.

My mother once joked that she'd like to have a baby on a Thursday just to see if Dad would miss going to press. But all three of his children cooperated with him; not one of his daughters was born on Thursday. In fact, my youngest sister, Joan, arrived a few minutes after midnight on Jan. 1 so Dad could rush home from the hospital and print New Year's greeting birth announcements.

Mother's kidding was in fun, though. She spent many years at Dad's side writing news items, proofreading and managing to buy

In the back of the room of the The Kansas Optimist, *owner and publisher Walter Carlile's wife, Lulu, worked on the Linotype. The copy was typed in and reproduced in hot lead. The hot lead would come out in lines, blocked together in a printer's frame.*

groceries during the Depression. Sometimes farm families paid for their subscriptions with eggs, a frying chicken or home-churned butter.

One year Dad decided not to print the usual letters to Santa Claus. He knew the children would be disappointed at not seeing their letters in print, but not nearly as disappointed as they would be when their parents couldn't afford to buy the toys and goodies they wanted. He told us he didn't want to be part of the heartache those parents would feel.

I don't remember how old I was when I first started "working" at the office. I'm sure I was less help than hindrance at first. A boy who worked around a newspaper office was called the "printer's devil." I beamed when Dad said a girl would be a "printer's angel." He also joked that he was the only man on Main Street who could hold his secretary on his lap and his wife wouldn't even care!

Dad used a Linotype for setting the news in type, but he set the ads by hand. I watched, fascinated, as his chubby fingers fairly flew, picking up one letter after another from the type case's little partitions. They clicked on the metal composing stick he held in his hand. He knew his p's and q's, all right. Although they looked backward when I saw them in type, they were correct on the printed page.

One of my jobs was "catching the papers" as they came off the old flatbed press. It automatically lifted the printed pages out onto a big, low table. I sat on a chair with sawed-off legs at just the right height for the low table. It wasn't a high-speed press. I had time to ease each page onto the pile of printed papers on the table, matching the edges as I stacked them.

(It wasn't until years later that I discovered there really wasn't much chance of those pages sliding onto the floor, even if I hadn't been sitting there to "catch" them.)

As the last copy was printed and the press ground to a halt, Dad would wave at me and call out, "I found it!"

"Found what?" I shouted back, knowing the answer. It was a corny, but dear little joke we shared.

"The bottom of the pile!" Dad would answer with a grin as he stepped down from the press.

It was a proud day for me when Dad called out from the back shop, "Phone the elevator for the market report." The report was a last-minute list of the current prices of wheat, corn, etc., for our front page. I felt like he was giving me a great responsibility. I knew the market report was the first thing farmers looked at when they took *The Kansas Optimist* from the mailbox.

Dad loved politics, and on election night, he kept the *Optimist* office open until midnight, if necessary, for election returns.

I remember how important I felt the year Wilkie ran against Roosevelt. I stayed at headquarters in the county seat 11 miles away, and as the reports came in, I telephoned Dad back in the printing office. I visualized myself as a real reporter!

It was a sad day when Dad told us he'd sold *The Optimist*. We were sitting at Sunday dinner when Dad, with his fondness for the dramatic, made his announcement. My sister Joan, who

had followed me as his "printer's angel," rushed out in tears. It was almost like losing a member of the family. Worse yet, it was doctor's orders. My father had Parkinson's disease.

Dad "sold" *The Optimist* two or three more times, taking it back each time. He said he couldn't "sell the town down the river." One buyer, a young city man, just could not fit in with small-town life. He locked the door at noon on Saturday! Didn't he know the farmers came to town on Saturday night and might stop by to pay their subscriptions, or just to talk awhile? Another man simply could not make it pay, even though *The Optimist* had kept a family going for more than 30 years. Finally a buyer hung on and *The Kansas Optimist* continued even after Dad died.

I can still remember the day my husband, Paul, came in and found me in tears, *The Optimist* in my hand. "Who died?" he asked, knowing that I always read the news about people in my hometown.

"*The Optimist!*" I sobbed. "That editor is giving up!" The page-one announcement explained the reasons—rising costs, trend of the times, competition of the city and so on. *The Kansas Optimist* was now another weekly newspaper on the long list of those that just couldn't make it.

Although Dad had been gone for a long time, it seemed to me that a part of him died again that day. But our memories of those happy times together at *The Kansas Optimist* will live on always. ✩

In the press room of The Kansas Optimist, *the Chandler paper cutter stands ready to trim printed reams of paper, the Kluge printing press, left of counter, is idle for the moment while editor-publisher Carlile works on copy. Behind him are the galley tables where the "printer's angel" worked.*

The Country Editor

By Harold Kolb

The editor of the weekly newspaper in a small Midwestern town was also the local postmaster when I worked there in the early part of the 20th century ago.

He was addicted to poker playing, fishing and a corncob pipe, but not necessarily in that order. He published the paper at regular intervals, more or less—when his other interests did not interfere.

The paper consisted of four pages of local news plus four pages of "patent insides." These were preprinted by the paper supply house and shipped every week.

The editor was rather indifferent about the paper's makeup. One week as I was making up the paper, I asked him what he wanted on the front page. "Put anything you want to on page one," he replied. "That ain't the question. The question is, where's my pipe?"

Our equipment included few cases of type, a rebuilt Linotype, a job press and an ancient cylinder press for printing the paper. The cylinder press was powered by a gasoline engine. Its exhaust pipe protruded through the wall, pointing toward the church across the block.

One Sunday evening we were belatedly printing the edition. The staccato bark of the gas engine's exhaust rang sharply in the still winter air. Suddenly the front door burst open and the Methodist minister strode in, Bible in one hand, hymnbook in the other and blood in his eye.

"If you're going to continue with this racket, I'll dismiss my Sunday-evening class at the church," he declared angrily. Then, turning on his heel, he stalked out.

"The parson seems pretty upset," the boss observed. "Maybe we'd better stop." The press run was nearly over anyway, and by the time the minister reached his church, quiet had been restored.

One week when time had hung on my hands, this item appeared in the paper: "Due to a breakdown of the motor which runs our press, local births, deaths and weddings will be postponed until next week." The boss didn't seem very happy about the line, and I pretended ignorance as to its origin.

But even the boss wasn't immune to humorous bouts with his readership. Many years ago many housewives baked bread at home. One week my country editor contributed this little gem for the edition:

"It has been reported that one of the fastidious young brides in town kneads bread with her gloves on. The editor of this paper needs bread with his shirt on, needs bread with his shoes on, he needs bread with his pants on, and unless some of the delinquent subscribers to this old rag of freedom pony up before long, he'll need bread without a darn thing on. And the Midwest is no Garden of Eden in the wintertime." ✯

Clicks in the Depot Window

By Chester Wesman

The "uptown" of our little Minnesota city was a dusty, three-block-long street across the railway tracks from our house. Two paths led to it. One followed a dirt trail through tall grass and passed the blacksmith shop; the other went by way of the railway depot. Both required crossing the tracks, a serious move made only with my mother's permission.

Our depot, like thousands of others in small towns all over the country, was a wooden building next to the tracks with a platform between the building and the rails. The middle of the building was the office, one end of which

was a telegraph operator's bay, bulging out toward the track. Seated at his desk, with telegraph instruments and train order blanks within easy reach, the operator had a clear view of the tracks in both directions.

Inside the office, a ticket window on one side opened into the women's waiting room, and a similar window on the opposite side served the men's waiting room. Adjacent to the latter was the freight house, an unheated storage room for freight waiting to be picked up. It also housed the high-wheeled hand trucks that were used to load and unload railway express parcels. Potbellied stoves fueled with huge chunks of soft coal kept the office and waiting rooms warm in winter.

Between the depot and the track was the platform of wood planking with crushed cinder extensions on each end.

As a barefoot boy on the way to town, I avoided the sharp cinders and walked gingerly across the wooden planks, trying not to stub a toe or pick up a splinter. I always heard the mysterious clicking of the telegraph instruments, even when nobody was there. The walls seemed to act as a sounding board, amplifying the sound. Sometimes when the depot was closed, I would press my nose against the bay window and peer between the papers hanging on hooks to see where the clicks came from. I knew that our neighbor who worked there could get messages from faraway places. Otherwise, he seemed like an ordinary person.

When I was 10, I swapped books with another boy, thereby acquiring a copy of the *Boy Scout Handbook*. It contained the International Morse Code as well as the Navy semaphore flag alphabet. My mother sewed black and white cloth triangles together to make a pair of signal flags and I tacked them onto a pair of sticks for handles. Waving the flags and frequently consulting the book, we sent messages to each other across the kitchen.

But the lure of the code was stronger. We memorized it and wrote each other notes in dots and dashes at every opportunity. Cuddled together on cold winter evenings, one of us would use a finger to press long and short characters into the other's palm.

In the late 1920s, a telephone construction crew came through town, leaving behind many small pieces of thin copper wire. I collected enough to twist together a telegraph line from our kitchen to the house of the boy next door. We used doorbells with the clappers cut off and foolishly connected the arrangement to regular 110-volt house current, fortunately escaping electrocution. We set out to learn the code, stuttering through important messages like, "Come on over."

One evening, my buzzer went wild with surprisingly rapid code accompanied by considerable smoke from the coils of the doorbell. A few minutes later, my friend came over with a visiting cousin, who had been the sender. He suggested that if I was interested in sending code, I should become a radio ham. Hams, he said, sent code messages to each other all over the world. I hadn't heard of ham radio before, but if it involved dots and dashes, I knew it was for me.

I sent away for a real telegraph key and my mother, always there to help and encourage me, learned to send code with it so I could practice receiving. Eventually I took the Federal Communications test and got my amateur license.

I was fascinated by radio and loved communicating with other hams using the international telegraph code. I wondered where I could get a job using a telegraph key. Then I remembered the clicking instruments in the depot.

Our depot was manned by the agent, Tom, during the day, and the telegraph operator, Leo, from 4 p.m. to midnight. Leo's shift was referred to as "second trick." I asked Tom if he would let me hang around as an unpaid helper to learn how to be an operator, and he graciously agreed. Then began what turned out to be nine months of intensive apprenticeship under Tom and Leo's generous tutelage.

I had to learn how to make out weekly and monthly reports not only for the railway, but also for the Railway Express Co. and the Western Union Telegraph Co. Each of these companies paid the agent a separate commission based on its business.

I spent my evenings with Leo patiently sending code to me, usually from a magazine story, and me copying it on a mill, operator jargon for typewriter—in this case, a No. 5 Underwood. I was glad I had taken typing in high school.

However, the American Morse Code used by "land-line" telegraph was not the same as international radio code. Many of the characters were different, better adapted to the clicking of a telegraph sounder.

The radio code came in shrill long and short whistles, more suitable for listening on the air where a signal might be very weak or there might be static or other interference. After a period of confusion, my ears untangled the codes, and from then on I could switch from one to the other at will.

Our depot, like thousands of others in small towns all over the country, was a wooden building next to the tracks with a platform between the building and the rails.

Train orders and the *Book of Rules* were important parts of my apprenticeship. I spent many cold winter evenings basking in the warmth of a potbellied stove, poring over the manual with Leo, and discussing the proper handling of various situations relating to train movements. On a single-track railroad, with trains running in both directions, a rigid set of rules was necessary for safe operation.

Which train had the right-of-way? Which would take the siding? We gave the rules a thorough going-over, posing every possible combination of circumstances. My ultimate employment as a telegrapher would depend not only on my ability to telegraph, but also on my ability to pass the *Book of Rules* test.

Our telegraph wires ran on pole lines to regional places of concentration call "relay" offices. These employed large numbers of telegraphers who relayed messages between cities that had no other direct connection.

Railway relay offices handled interoffice company messages and were located at the railway headquarters and in cities where the company had divisional offices. In relay offices, the operators did nothing but send and receive messages. There was no station accounting to do. Since my first love was telegraphing, or "pounding brass," as it was called in reference to the brass key, I resolved to someday work in a relay office.

The Great Northern Railway had 11 relay offices with about 112 operators. The largest offices, in St. Paul and Seattle, each employed about 25 telegraphers. Commercial telegraph companies such as Western Union and Postal Telegraph had their own relay offices in major cities. The actual commercial wires, however, generally were on the railway pole lines under an agreement.

During the heyday of telegraph, the main Western Union relay office in New York employed 600 telegraphers in one room, while the company's Chicago relay office employed more than 300 telegraphers in one room. The wooden floor had smooth polished pathways where the "check kids" roller-skated between rows of tables from one wire position to another, distributing hard copies of received messages.

A telegram to be relayed was first hung on a hook by a receiving operator. Then it was picked up and carried to an operator who was sending to the destination. Messages for delivery in the city were given to a messenger boy or sent by pneumatic tube to a branch office to be carried by messenger from there.

When I lived in Chicago for two years as a boy, I had admired the ubiquitous khaki-uniformed Western Union messenger boys on bicycles, with folded messages sticking out from under their caps, as they nonchalantly maneuvered through snarled traffic. I longed to be one of them.

The following spring, Tom said I was ready to apply for a job. I wrote letters to every division on the railroad and waited to hear. The first favorable response came from Superior, Wis,, headquarters of the Mesabi Division. It was 1937; Europe was arming for war and the demand for Minnesota's iron ore was great, so we were busy.

Eventually I worked at many places on the Great Northern, and I did get into the relay service. After a few happy years, I decided that telegraphy was not going to last much longer and I had better move on. Consequently, I took a night shift in Seattle and went to college during the day to get a degree in electrical engineering.

Ultimately, telegraphy was edged out by the Teletype machine, and that in turn gave way to the computer. It is hard to imagine now the thousands of telegraph jobs that existed during the heyday of Morse. Before long-distance telephone was widespread, the "information highway" consisted of a web of telegraph wires crisscrossing the nation. Newspapers had telegraphers in their editorial offices. Sportswriters traveled with personal telegraphers who sent the stories on a direct wire to the newsroom as they were written.

Associated Press and other news services leased their own wires and had their own telegraphers. At important trials, courtroom telegraphers were equipped with silent sounders, tiny instruments in earpieces, to avoid disturbing the court. From there news was flashed to newspaper editors.

Wires from the New York Stock Exchange ran to stockbrokers all over the country, and stock transactions were handled by tele-graphers. Many thousands of telegraphers were needed, and it was easy for an operator to get a job.

A class of roving telegraphers called "boom-ers" developed. These free-spirited operators moved about the country at will, working a job for a little while before moving on.

The depot where I first heard the clicks as a small boy and apprentice is gone now, as are the shining rails that once ran in front of it and the pole-line with its cross arms full of wire. At one time, the goods of the world had come to us on those rails, and the news of the world on those wires.

Ever since the dawn of civilization, man has struggled to overcome time and distance. The telegraph conquered both with the touch of an operator's finger. Oh, how I still miss those clicks in the depot window! ☆

Red on 2, Green on 4

By John H. Mahan

"Red on 2, green on 4, yellow on line 2," was a little jingle I had to learn the summer of 1913, when I was learning to be a telephone installer. I was delighted to get the job, especially since I was studying electrical engineering at the University of Pennsylvania. This would help me learn the practical side.

In those days New Jersey didn't have its own company. The Bell Telephone Co. of Pennsylvania from Philadelphia serviced Princeton and points south. The part of New Jersey north of Princeton came under the direction of The New York Telephone Co., headquartered in New York City. I was living in Trenton, N.J., where the phone company had a storeroom and headquarters for its installation force, on Ferry Street near North Broad.

I was assigned to help an installer named George Fletcher. He seemed pleased to have me and gradually showed me how to go about installing a phone. I helped carry the bag of tools and watched carefully, handing him a tool, pulling in a wire and so on, until the phone was in place. One thing I remember about George: His left hand was missing the three inner fingers, leaving just the thumb and little finger. I never asked him how it happened and he never spoke about it, but it didn't seem to handicap him in his work.

We had a good supervisor by the name of Rogotsky, a large man with a round face, who wore glasses. He had been sent up from Philadelphia. As an incentive to the installers to learn more about their work, he volunteered

to conduct a class on Thursday evenings from 7–9 p.m. Before class he always prepared a piece of telephone equipment with some defect in it—perhaps a broken wire, incorrect wiring or a defective part. Then we were supposed to locate the trouble. These exercises proved to be very interesting and helpful.

After I had been helping George Fletcher for several weeks, the supervisor came around and whispered in my ear, "Do you think you could put in a phone by yourself?"

This frightened me; I was quite sure I couldn't, so I said, "No, not yet." However he kept asking, and I finally said, "I'll try."

My first assignment was a residence in the Cadwalader section of Trenton. Here is what it took: a coil of three-conductor wire, a piece of tubing, my bag of tools, a bell box, a desk stand phone and a protector—quite a load to carry. In the bag of tools was a test set: a brace, a long shank bit, a file, a tack hammer, several screwdrivers, a pair of wire cutters, a pair of diagonal pliers and a pair of long-nose pliers; also a star drill, a short-handled sledgehammer, sandpaper, some nails, round screws, fiber cleats and a pocketknife. For transportation I had 5 cents trolley fare. All in all, it was quite an impressive collection.

I took the West State Street trolley, got off and found the house. A lady answered the doorbell and showed me where she wanted the phone in the dining room. I unloaded my things and took a look down in the cellar. Then I looked around outside, where I found where the drop loop gang had run a wire from the pole to the side of the house and down to just over a cellar window. With my brace and bit I bored a hole in the window frame, slanted upward, installed the fuse and lightning protector on the cellar beams near the window, inserted a piece of tubing and fed the loop wires inside, leaving a drip loop so the rain would drop off and not run inside. Then I connected the loop wires to the protector and ran a ground wire to clamp on a water pipe. Next, moving upstairs, I bored a hole in the dining-room floor and ran my three-conductor wire from the dining room to the protector in the cellar. So far, so good.

Now I had only to mount the bell box on the dining-room wall, check it with a pocket level, set the desk-stand phone on a table and connect everything—the three-conductor wire, the phone cord and the bell box. Here's where the jingle came in: "Red on 2, green on 4, yellow on line 2."

You see, the three-conductor wire had a tracer thread in each wire—one red, one green and one yellow. The terminals on the equipment were numbered 2, 4 and line 2. So I connected everything up, took off the receiver and listened.

Nothing. Everything was dead.

Now I was *sure* I wasn't ready to install a phone. I hoped the lady of the house wasn't watching. Taking my test set, I went outside and connected it to the drop loop wires and called the test table. They were very helpful. They must have known I was a novice and questioned me very carefully as to just how I had connected the wires. Following their instructions, I went back inside and found where I had made a mistake. This time when I lifted the receiver, the operator answered and

After I had been helping George Fletcher for several weeks, the supervisor came around and whispered in my ear, "Do you think you could put in a phone by yourself?"

I asked to be connected to the test table. I asked them to give me a ring and I hung up. The phone rang. I acknowledged it and notified the lady of the house that her phone was ready to use.

The rest of that summer, I installed phones without any further trouble. Then came Easter vacation from college, and I was again given a job—but this time "shooting trouble," which meant going out on service calls when something went wrong and the phone wouldn't work. One of these phones was in the office of Woodrow Wilson, president of Princeton University (before he became president of the United States). My previous training by my supervisor, Mr. Rogotsky, helped me locate a defective condenser in the bell box. Once this was changed, the phone worked.

Another assignment was in the State Home for Epileptics in Skillman, outside Princeton. The Princeton wire chief drove me over to Skillman in his Ford runabout. We went on an inspection tour of the whole village. The village had installed their own wiring and equipment and then asked the Bell Co. to be connected to their lines. We soon found out that their installation was quite haphazard—wires with poor insulation, run in a careless manner, not at all like the careful way that was standard Bell practice. The only way they could expect good service was to completely overhaul their wiring—rip out here, replace there—either doing it themselves or having the Bell Co. do it.

My experience as an installer will always remain a pleasant memory in a fascinating and ever-changing industry. ✦

A Century of the Telephone

Through the Great Depression, a struggling telephone industry crept along with advancing technology. In 1940, progress stopped as most personnel and materials were used to fight and win World War II. In 1945 the boys came home and the baby boom began. Telephones were in demand, and like many cities across the country, Paducah, Ky., added switchboards and equipment. Installing and maintaining two copper wires from the switching office to each telephone in the community, plus adding many long-distance trunk circuits to other towns, were unending tasks. This mural, "A Century of the Telephone" by artist Robert Dafford was painted on the Paducah, flood wall in 2000.

Telephone Service, Country Style

By Nadine Butler

This morning I direct-dialed a call to Paris from Wisconsin. How could a woman who began her career as a telephone operator in 1931 *not* be impressed? If we could have imagined then the wonders of today's phone systems, we would have thought we were dreaming.

Our service was fine as it was. Big, durable, wooden phones were mounted on the wall, with a crank on the side for signaling the operator, a heavy black receiver for listening, and a mouthpiece for sending out our voice. In towns as small as the one where I grew up, there was also the friendly operator. We knew by her voice whether it was Pearl or Blanche or Hattie. Who needed more?

On special occasions when a long-distance call was needed, we had only to give the operator the name and address of the person to whom we wished to talk, and she called us back when she had reached our party. Simple. And being a telephone operator was a cut above some other jobs that women could hold.

In 1931, the Great Depression was still known only as "hard times." Jobs were scarce, but in my first year out of high school I was one of the lucky people to find one, as a telephone operator! My tour of duty in that respected occupation lasted only five months, but it left a trail of memories.

The 700 people in our village, plus a prosperous farming community, were served by two phone companies: the old, established one with its fine, up-to-date office of The Big Telephone Co. on Main Street, and the much smaller Dekorra Farmers Telephone Co.

In April 1931 I went to work for the Farmers Co. Its whole operation was run from a small frame house on a side street. Inside the front door was a family living room. To the left, in a sunny alcove with a big bay window, was the tall black switchboard with its high swivel stool, winking lights and connecting plugs in a bristling row at the front.

The live-in operator-bookkeeper was a pleasant woman named Mrs. Lyons. Hers was a 24-hour-a-day responsibility. In return she received living quarters in the house for herself and two young daughters, plus 25 cents an hour. From that wage she was expected to pay someone to relieve her at the switchboard a few hours a day. A bell awakened her for nighttime calls.

My wage as her helper was to be 12 cents an hour for 20 hours a week. Every two weeks I would take home a check for $4.80. But it was only a half-time job, and as the going rate was $1 per day for inexperienced people like me, the wage was satisfactory. There were fringe benefits, too. I had the satisfaction of using those wonderful phrases, "going to work" and "my job." And, as my mother said, it was "dignified work."

Mrs. Lyons explained the switchboard operation. I put on the headset, and when a light flashed on the board, I inserted a plug and said, crisply and pleasantly, "Number, please," and "Thank you," just as I had heard it all my life. It was heady stuff for a 17-year-old.

Most phones in town were on three or four party lines, but stretching miles of wire from farm to farm was expensive and one line in the country sometimes had as many as 20 phones. That meant a long list of ring combinations to learn: a long and two shorts, three shorts and two longs, and so on. A call to one home rang in all homes on the line. *Click, click* on the line meant that neighbors were also quietly lifting their receivers to listen. Not much could be done about this "rubbering," as we called it, except to be careful what one said.

But there was a good side to it, too. In an emergency one could ring one or two neighbors and say, for example, "There's a fire at the Smith farm on Highway K." If half a dozen ears were listening, help would be on the way.

Neighbors learned about accidents, who was ill, who had died or had a baby. The real hazard of the big party line was the occasional woman who couldn't resist long social visits. Sometimes she had to be told by her neighbors to get off the line so someone else could use it.

It was when Mrs. Lyons explained the procedure for fire calls that anxiety struck.

"When a fire call comes," she said, "get the name and address and repeat it before you disconnect." She went to a small black box on the wall. "Then pull this lever down and the siren will start."

The siren was on the roof of the village hall. I knew that at its first low moan, volunteer firemen would leave their work or their dinner tables or their beds, and by the time it had "revved up" to its screaming wail, those men would be speeding toward the firehouse. The first one there would phone and say, "Where's the fire?" Around town, some people would hurry out to the road to see which direction the fire truck went. Others would call the operator to ask where the fire was, and the sudden burst of calls would, I was sure, light the switchboard like a Christmas tree. Receivers on party lines would go up and soon dozens of people would know where the fire was. It was an enormous responsibility—and it rested squarely on my shoulders!

The what-ifs began to haunt me. What if the caller was too excited to be understood? What if I became flustered and forgot? What if a house burned down because of me? The little black box hung there, threatening.

Then one day it happened! A voice bearing only a thin edge of anxiety said, "Would you please call the fire department? Our grass fire is getting away from us." It was all perfectly clear. With shaking hand and pounding heart, I pulled the handle on the black box. I had passed the first crisis of my working life.

I was so shaken, however, that I also committed my first real blunder. My fumbling fingers somehow sent a long, loud ring into the ear of a woman who was talking. Her opinion of me, delivered in colorful language a couple of minutes later, was neither charitable nor forgiving.

The Big Co. and the Farmers Co. had a unique problem. Never was there a wire connecting the two switchboards. The only way a subscriber of one company could call a number of the other company was to have the call routed in a long-distance loop to town 12 miles away. From there it was returned as a toll call. It meant also that businesses, doctors and ministers had to have both phones.

One shortcut was used a few times by our subscribers. "Will you do me a favor?" a voice asked sweetly one day. "On your way home, will you stop at Maggie Wilson's and ask her to call me?" Maggie, I knew, had a Big Co. phone, but she could step across the street to use the Farmers Co. phone in a store.

We operators provided other services. "I'm going to be at Mother's today," a caller might say. "If I have any calls, ring me there." In this little town, we knew most people—*and* their relations.

All operators gave custom service to the doctor. "Send my calls to the cottage," he'd say when he wanted to get away for a few hours at his cabin on the lake.

One day an exasperated mother called from a block up the street. "Johnnie's run away again. Would you look out the window and see if you see him?" I looked, but Johnnie apparently had headed in another direction.

On afternoons when there were few calls, Mrs. Lyons suggested that I turn on the night bell and sit in the living room and read. Sometimes the warm aroma of supper cooking wafted in from the kitchen, and the Lyons girls came home full of schoolgirl fun. I liked my job.

But in September the opportunity came to step up to a full-time position in the local general store at $6 a week. No one could turn down an offer like that.

The homey kind of telephone service that small-town America once knew, with its person-to-person touch and its operators we knew by name and voice, is gone. As well as it worked for us then, it is too costly and too slow for today.

Several years ago the evening news told about the closing of a little telephone company in rural New England. Pictures showed a switchboard in what appeared to be a private home. It was thought, the commentator said, to be the last one in the United States. Our country-style telephone service is now unquestionably part of the Good Old Days. ✩

The Internet's Grandfather

By Bill Siuru

"Surfing the Web" on a computer is both entertaining and mind expanding. While surfing and downloading information from the Internet the other evening, I remembered how I tuned in on the entire world years ago, before computers were invented. Back then, I was an avid shortwave listener, or "SWL" for short.

At about the age of 8, I discovered shortwave radio when I dialed the large Zenith in our living room to the shortwave bands. (In those days, radios included exotic names like London, Paris, Rome and Tokyo printed on the large dials.) World War II was ending and the broadcasts were filled with news about the war and the forthcoming peace.

For the next few years I had a passing interest in shortwave radio. However, by my early teen years, I really was hooked. I spent hours at the library poring over *The Amateur Radio Handbook* as well as radio and electronics magazines. I even acquired vacuum tubes, condensers, resistors and so forth to build a simple shortwave radio, which required earphones.

Today, e-mail, chat rooms and news groups allow people to communicate with others around the world on a one-to-one basis. The equivalents back then were the amateur radio bands used by the hams. While voice transmissions were becoming popular, much of the interchange was still by Morse Code.

Indeed, in order to get an amateur license from the FCC that allowed you to transmit messages rather than just receive, you had to take a test to show your proficiency in Morse Code. I never got beyond the novice class. Some hams were so good that they could not only send and receive at lightning speed, they could actually identify who was doing the sending by the person's "touch" on the telegraph key.

Hams were much more civilized. Unlike the Internet, there was absolutely no X-rated material. Indeed, your license could be yanked by the FCC if you even transmitted a naughty word.

For my 30th birthday I got a neat Hallicrafters shortwave radio. I believe it cost $39.95. Compared with my homemade equipment, it was the equivalent of a state-of-the-art personal computer. Its reception was much better than my homemade radio's.

Unlike the Internet, on which everything is digitally clear whether it originates across town or halfway around the world, shortwave radio transmission from faraway places depended on whether "the skip was in." Radio beams are reflected or "bounced" off the earth's ionosphere. Amateurs and SWLs were usually night owls since reception was far better after dark. But even then, signals faded in and out and were interspersed with whistles, static and crackling.

When I tired of listening to the dots and dashes, I tuned in to news from the BBC in London, music from Radio Brazzaville in the Belgian Congo, Radio Moscow's propaganda or religion from the "Voice of the Andes" in Quito, Ecuador. I listened in on transmissions between ships at sea, police and fire calls, and pilots talking to the tower. There was always something of interest.

I collected DX (long distance reception) cards that proved I had actually heard particular broadcasting stations. When I heard a broadcast I sent a postcard to the address given. A few weeks later, I received a DX card, which usually had a postcard picture of the locale, station call letters, and a foreign stamp to add to my collection. The walls of my "radio shack" in my bedroom were soon covered with DX cards from around the world.

Unlike the Internet with its great graphics, DX cards were the only graphic component of shortwave radio. Everything else had to be visualized in the mind. ✩

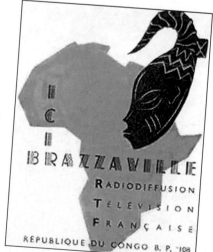

A 1959 DX card from Radio Brazzaville in the Belgian Congo.

Radio: The Early Decades

By Paul F. Long

*D*o you remember the first radio program you were privileged to hear? Surely that was a magical moment, when sound and exciting entertainment were first brought over the airwaves by the miraculous technology of the early 20th century.

Our first fascinating encounter with this new entertainment medium occurred something less than a decade after 1920, when radio programming was begun. The latter 1920s were times of economic deprivation; few homes had radios. But one of our more-affluent neighbors had acquired one of the newfangled instruments and invited friends for an evening of entertainment. The program was *Amos 'n' Andy*, and we listened to the hilarious dialogue of Freeman Gosden and Charles Correll in awed wonder.

With that introduction to electric communications, our world was forever changed.

It would still be several years before we purchased our first radio, but we were fortunate to have an older brother who had some knowledge of electric circuitry and a talent for tinkering. From old radio tubes, condensers, filaments and resisters scavenged from discarded radios or given to him, he built a radio.

We lived in the country before rural electrification, so the power was furnished by "B" batteries, large dry-cell batteries. The aerial was copper wire, some hundred feet or more, which ran from the upstairs bedroom window to a pole planted in the garden.

At first, due in part to the weak signal, earphones were necessary to hear the programs. Ultimately a speaker was added, and the home-made radio was moved to the living room to be shared by our family.

The powerful "X stations," or "border

For a brief interval, it appeared that television might mean the end of radio. But such was not the case.

stations," probably did more to popularize radio and country music (first known as "hillbilly music") than any other factor. In 1922 some 510 radio stations were broadcasting across the United States. Of these, 89 were located in the South, 25 in Texas alone. The rural, more-insular South had long been the bastion of country music, and so the music broadcast by those stations was predominantly country. This was true especially of the X stations.

The individual who inaugurated the X stations was a displaced Kansan, Dr. J.R. Brinkley. He had formerly operated a radio station at Milford, Kan., which he used to push goat-gland operations that purportedly renewed sexual potency. During his run for Kansas governor in 1930, Brinkley featured hillbilly performers at his campaign rallies.

Shortly after Brinkley's radio license was revoked in Kansas, he moved his operation to Del Rio, Texas, and began X-station broadcasting. It was probably only natural that he featured hillbilly music on his programs, the recordings scattered in a sea of advertising.

Largely unregulated with regard to transmitter power and the near-fraudulent claims made by advertisers, the X stations beamed across North America and reached a great many listeners. With their powerful signals, the X stations nearly dominated nighttime radio. We spent many evenings listening and soon became acquainted with a variety of patented potions and nostrums that claimed to heal every ill imaginable, plus some unimaginable ones. In essence, the X stations became the medicine shows of the airwaves.

Not only did they offer cures for ailments, but also treatments to beautify and enhance: "color black" to dye the hair, hair-restoring nostrums, an amazing variety of cough syrups (reportedly rich in alcohol), and numerous elixirs to pep up tired blood.

In addition, veterinarian needs and all manner of botanical items could be ordered through the mail. These offers and countless others were pushed, the ads interspersed with a minimum of entertainment programming.

A good number of these stations beamed their programs to predominantly rural audiences in the South, the Southwest and Midwest. For our family and for people all across America, hillbilly music was *our* music. Much of it was derived from the folk music originally brought from Northern Europe by early immigrants.

Gradually, this music was amalgamated with blues, jazz and Western ballads and became what was first known as "country" (a designation given hillbilly music in 1949 by *Billboard Magazine*), and finally "country-western" music. Country and country-western music became extremely popular in the United States and around the world.

At first, radio programming brought a great reduction in recording and record sales. But this gradually changed as radio entertainers gained a following and created a demand for their recordings. The increasing popularity of the jukebox also encouraged record sales. Remember those beautifully lit, glitzy machines that played a favorite recording for a nickel?

Another stimulant for record production was the use of recordings for broadcasting; this was especially true with the border stations. In turn, sales of phonographs increased.

Throughout the 1930s and well into the 1940s, the names of many country stars became household names in America, even worldwide. Some of our favorite country artists were Roy Acuff, Bill Monroe, the Carter Family, Ernie Tubbs, and Bob Wills and the Texas Playboys.

The Saturday-night "barn dance" radio programs were an entertainment phenomenon of that era. They offered several hours of entertainment. Notable among these was the *National Barn Dance* out of Chicago, presented by WLS, the station operated by Sears, Roebuck and Co. as a service to its farm customers.

Other well-known Saturday-night "hoedowns" were *The Grand Ole Opry*, originating from Nashville; WWVA's *Jamboree* from Wheeling, W.Va., and *Louisiana Hayride* from KWKH in Shreveport, La.

On Saturday nights I stayed up listening to these programs into the wee hours, repeatedly assuring my father, who had plans for my working the following day, that I would go to bed "in a little while."

The tremendously popular artists whose hits were heard over and over via radio and jukeboxes are especially memorable for those who remember the World War II years. In the bars, pool halls and restaurants in towns near military bases, and in the PXs on the bases themselves, jukeboxes toiled far into the night.

I recall that *New San Antonio Rose* by Bob Wills and the Texas Playboys, *Walking the Floor Over You* by Texan Ernie Tubbs, and *Wabash Cannonball* performed by Roy Acuff were played endlessly by homesick GIs.

The status of these radio country artists is noted in a story told by Ernie Pyle, famed World War II correspondent. According to Pyle, one Japanese battle cry was, "To h--- with Roosevelt, to h--- with Babe Ruth, to h--- with Roy Acuff!"

Another popular genre in radio programming in the 1930s and early 1940s was the comedy patterned after the pioneering *Amos 'n' Andy*. Some of the most popular of these shows were *The Bob Hope Show, The Red Skelton Show, The Fred Allen Program, The Jack Benny Show, Fibber McGee and Molly,* and *George Burns and Gracie Allen.*

For a brief interval, it appeared that television might mean the end of radio. But such was not the case. As comic Milton Berle quipped, "If radio could not kill radio, how could television kill radio?"

One can only wonder what the X Stations of the 1930s might have accomplished with modern technology, like satellites. Perhaps the Laplander tending his caribou on the barren stretches of northern Finland would have been dyeing his hair with Color Black, and going about his work singing Roy Acuff's *Wabash Cannonball.* ✬

The Miracle

By Bill Koester

At my friend Harry's house, four of us preteens huddled over a Mighty Midget radio, as fidgety as expectant fathers pacing in anticipation of their firstborn. When it was my turn, I quivered with excitement. I put on the earphones and heard an orchestra playing *In My Merry Oldsmobile*—my first radio reception. I marveled at the miracle. I begrudged the others their turns with the head-set. I was captivated by this creation that plucked sound from the atmosphere.

I craved a radio of my own. Harry's father, who owned an electrical-repair shop, had just stocked some radios and radio parts. My meager savings could purchase only the few parts and instructions needed to make the simplest crystal set, the poor man's radio.

My first radio had three main parts. First there was a tuner made from a Quaker Oats box squeezed between two squares of wood and wound with a skin of fine, lacquered copper wire and a brass bar and slide across the top. Then there was a pickup consisting of a galena crystal and a "cat's whisker"—a fine wire whose free end could be moved to contact any point on the surface of the crystal. Finally there was an earphone set.

After finishing the assembly one afternoon, I wolfed down my dinner and dashed from the table mouthing a hasty "'scuse me." My all-steel bedspring subbed as an antenna. I adjusted the cat's whisker to a firm contact with the crystal. Then, after donning the headset, I inched the slide along the wire path, holding my breath to hear a whisper. The slide reached the far end; I pushed it back, bit by bit. I shifted the cat's whisker and tried again and again. I was sweating. Was the bedspring OK? Was the wiring correct? It *had* to work! Wait! A sound? I moved the slide back ever so little. Music!

After trial-and-error positioning, the cat's whisker contacted a "live" spot on the crystal and the music of *The Glow Worm* filled my ears. I had never heard sweeter music. The announcer identified KYW, Chicago. Wow! I ran through the house, yelling, "KYW, Chicago!" I dragged my parents and sister to my room, dancing in delight as each tried the earphones and showed surprise.

That radio flip-flopped my life. It usurped my spare time; it lullabied me to sleep; it outranked my chores and homework until my parents exploded. It captured WWJ, Detroit, and on good nights pulled in KDKA, Pittsburgh, although the sound faded to nothingness periodically. It represented a metamorphosis in entertainment to me, but only a fad to Father and Mother.

By this time, Harry's living room sported an eight-tube Atwater Kent, a breathtaking beauty with tuners, tubes and accessories mounted on a bottom board and a shiny, black front panel with three large dials for tuning. I drooled. But back home, my parents quashed my obvious sales patter. The hand-wound phonograph that often played *Whispering Hope,* with Mom and Dad singing along, satisfied their entertainment needs, along with games of rummy and dominoes.

A one-tube set would sell them, I was sure, but I had no money. Then I lucked out, as one by one, the firemen in the firehouse next-door hired me to build crystal sets for them. I bought a one-tube kit with my earnings. The reception on the one-tube radio with an attic antenna was a vast improvement. With the earphones on the table, three of us could hear the program without straining. My dad was impressed, but he still dubbed it a fleeting fancy.

After months of cajoling, Dad finally caved in and we added a Crosley nine-tuber at Christmas that year. Yet, nothing will ever replace that wonderful moment when my first crystal set brought the world outside into our simple home.

Radio breathed freshness and fun into our lives. We laughed with it, we cried with it, we "yes'ed" it, we "no'ed" it, we shared Sunday supper with it. Radio was the miracle of my youth. ✯

A D-Day Prayer

By Brian C. Baur

*I*t was a bit unusual. We had just heard President Franklin D. Roosevelt the previous night—June 5, 1944—when he had told us about the fall of Rome the previous day. "The first of the Axis capitals is now in our hands," he had said. "One up and two to go."

Now FDR was on the air again. What news could he be bringing us so soon?

"My fellow Americans, last night, when I spoke with you about the fall of Rome, I knew at that moment that troops of the United States and our allies were crossing the channel in another and greater operation. It has come to pass with success thus far." So that was it! All Allied forces were crossing the English Channel onto the European continent at last.

Then the president asked all the people listening to him to join him in prayer: "Almighty God, our sons, pride of our nation, this day have set upon a mighty endeavor, a struggle to preserve our republic, our religion and our civilization, and to set free a suffering humanity."

Tears flowed freely in our home, as I'm sure they did in homes throughout the nation on that summer day. Mostly, however, they were tears of joy.

Every head in our home was bowed, every hand clasped tightly. This wasn't just a speech; this was something that came from deep within the president, and it touched deep within all who heard it. He was talking about brothers, fathers and sons.

"They will need Thy blessings. Their road will be long and hard, for the enemy is strong. He may hurl back our forces. Success may not come with rushing speed, but we shall return again and again; and we know that by Thy grace, and by the righteousness of our cause, our sons will triumph."

The president spoke slowly and deliberately. We could see him in our minds' eyes, sitting in the White House, hands clasped, head bowed, feeling what the families of all the fighting men were feeling at that moment.

"These men are lately drawn from the ways of peace. They fight not for the lust of conquest. They fight to end conquest. They fight to liberate. They fight to let justice arise, and tolerance and good-will among all Thy people. They yearn but for the end of battle, for their return to the haven of home. Some will never return. Embrace these, Father, and receive them, Thy heroic servants, into Thy kingdom."

Tears flowed freely in our home, as I'm sure they did in homes throughout the nation on that summer day. Mostly, however, they were tears of joy. The Allies were advancing now. Their indomitable will would not be stopped.

"Many people have urged that I call the nation into a single day of special prayer, but because the road is long and the desire is great, I ask that our people devote themselves in a continuance of prayer. As we rise to each new day, and again when each day is spent, let words of prayer be on our lips, invoking Thy help to our efforts."

We could imagine the weight he bore as he awaited the results from Normandy.

"Give us strength, too— strength in our daily tasks, to redouble the contributions we make in physical and the material support of our armed forces.

"And, O Lord, give us Faith," the president beseeched, and even over the radio we knew that he had capitalized the first letter of the word. "Give us Faith in Thee; Faith in our sons; Faith in each other; Faith in our united

crusade. Let not the impacts of temporary events, of temporal matters of but fleeting moment—let not these deter us in our unconquerable purpose."

President Roosevelt asked all the people listening to him to join him in prayer … Every head in our home was bowed, every hand clasped tightly.

One could imagine the silence throughout the nation as its people listened and prayed along with their president and commander-in-chief.

"With Thy blessing," President Roosevelt concluded, "we shall prevail over the unholy forces of our enemy. Help us to conquer the apostles of greed and racial arrogancies. Lead us to the saving of our country and, with our sister nations, into a world unity that will spell a sure peace—a peace invulnerable to the schemings of unworthy men, and a peace that will let all men live in freedom, reaping the just rewards of their honest toil.

"Thy will be done, almighty God. Amen."

It was so typical of the man who had been our president for these 11 years that in the midst of an invasion that would forecast our ability to win this war—and while other lands were suppressing news and religion—he would be sharing the news from the European theater and praying along with us for its success. ✫

Saturday Night Was Always Live!

By Mary Jo Collins

I was 16 and I was scared. I had never seen a television studio, camera or director—but there I was, live, on the air, auditioning for a candy commercial during the Saturday-night 10 o'clock news.

The father of a school friend owned the candy store; he had written the copy and sent it with his daughter on Thursday. I had memorized it—but at that moment, I couldn't remember it, or my own name.

Mom had dropped me at the Channel 5 studio at 8 o'clock. I stood on the corner with tears rolling down the pancake makeup I hoped television people wore.

It seemed like a long walk from the curb to the impressive station with the towering antenna. I wasn't anxious to get there.

"Can I help you, Miss?"

The receptionist was a bleached blonde, skinny where she should be, looking like a perfect candy saleslady.

"I'm here to do a commercial on tonight's news."

She dialed the phone, said something softly and we waited. Maybe they'd forgotten. Maybe it was the wrong night. Maybe I could go home.

The door marked "Keep Out" opened.

"Come right in, Miss."

I followed him down the long row of closed doors to Studio B, which looked just like Gym 101 at school. In the concrete room was a 4-foot area lit from all directions. Two canvas walls with a sign, "Fanny Farmer," were angled behind a table filled with candies. A long piece of velvet covered the boxes and wooden blocks that propped the display.

"Stand on the masking tape. Don't move or you'll cover the sign or be out of the light. I'm glad you didn't wear white; causes a halo, you know."

I didn't know. I rejoiced in the oxford cloth blouse with the calico flower at the neck; it was old, comfortable and—thank heavens!—blue.

"Meet John on camera one, Pete on two. You ever do this before? That's what I thought. When the red light goes on, start. The camera will move in slowly till only your hands show. Tape your copy to the back of the box and read. Paragraph three is a close-up of you; look right into the big lens and smile. Let's give it a try."

"Stand by."

"I'm your friendly Fanny Farmer saleslady and I have some good news for you."

"Cut, cut—that means stop. They only sent one buttercream egg. Don't cut it till we're on the air. Be sure no chocolate goes in; we'll be on an extreme close-up."

"Sure," I said, wondering how you kept the chocolate from going in, wondering how you kept the knife from shaking.

"Good job. Go through it again if you want. Try to relax. There's coffee in the control room. Two hours to go. Do you want a boom or lavalier? The mike, I mean … do you want to wear it, or have it over your head? Give her a boom."

By 10 o'clock, George Gobel had waved goodbye, the newsman tried his smile, the weatherboard had been decorated and a wrestler was hovering over the guest chair at the sports desk. Then, from a hollow voice, came the command I dreaded: "Stand by."

I looked at the chocolate rabbit propped on five books; it was too close to the lights. The hollow bunny's front and back were straining to melt and meet.

"We're brought to you tonight by your good friends at Fanny Farmer."

I said to the big red eye, "I'm your friendly Fanny Farmer saleslady and I've some good news for you." I took the knife, steadying my hand on the table.

Please, chocolate, don't crumble in on the creamy white nougat and rich yellow center.

Camera two was so close that I could see myself in the lens. "For your convenience, these Fanny Farmer shops will be open tomorrow." The light went off; I read the addresses.

The chocolate bunny collapsed.

So did I.

That's the way it was in the Good Old Days.

My next job was as Checkerboard Hostess three days a week for Ralston Purina; still no auditions, no competition.

The modeling schools were sending pretty young things by 1956, but they had no experience in writing copy, calling camera shots or serving sponsors.

For Women Only was my daily radio show; *The Early Show With Mary Jo* was my daily television show. In addition, there were a children's show, interviews and the weather.

If the Magic Marker for my weatherboard was missing, I always knew where to look. Harry Reasoner's kids liked to draw pictures under Daddy's desk while he read the news.

Phyllis Diller, with her electric-shock hairdo, climbed onto my desk and flew off in her signature wacky style. She had just been discovered

A 1950s studio cameraman brings live television to the masses.

Charlton Heston as Moses.

on the old *Tonight Show* and was in town to promote her nightclub act. We shopped for feathers for her costume after the show.

Charlton Heston flexed his cheekbones and talked about Moses and his new movie *The Ten Commandments.* Betty Friedan hailed me as the perfect example of the liberated woman—and almost ruined my amateur standing. The opening night of Cinerama, my first remote, I was to interview Mitzi Gaynor! But Mitzi was ill so they sent a sub, a shy starlet with no last name—Ann Margret.

In the Good Old Days, I flew to Hollywood to appear in Chuck Connors' *The Rifleman* as a publicity promotion. For three days, I was due at the studio at 7 a.m. for make-up, costumes and rehearsal.

"More apple pie, sir?" was my line.

Chuck Connors said, "No thanks," but we made the cover of *TV Guide.*

Later, we broadcast daily from the Minnesota State Fair, where I was charmed by an orangutan, felt the milk vein of a golden Guernsey and became an expert on the kazoo.

We worked Christmas Day and New Year's Eve.

It was all live in 1959. Now there's video-tape—and minicams, meteorologists, idea girls, copywriters, producers. But they can't have more fun than we did in the 1950s, when television was young and so was I. ☆

Inspiring a Nation

★ ★ ★ ★ ★

As I sat at the big wooden table in my office, putting the finishing touches on this book, thinking about all the people that made (and make) this country great, I realized I wasn't done yet.

To this point we have had the stories of the common people who are the backbone of the greatest country on Earth. But many times leaders have stepped into the breach to help us vertebrae stay strong.

Whether they were soldiers or politicians, aviators or authors, humorists or moralists—these heroes inspired a nation to keep the faith, to never lose hope, to always keep a steady eye on the horizon and a steady hand at the helm.

So often overcoming so much in their own lives, they inspired us to keep moving forward, even when the craggy mountain of life seemed too steep to climb.

So, I called Janice to that old wooden table and we assembled this representative group of national inspiration. We realize that hundreds of others deservedly could be added to this chapter. We hope this short list of 20th century icons serves only as a reminder of *all* those great men and women who served us, protected us, educated us, humored us—yes, and *inspired* us. We are a better nation because of them.

—Ken Tate

Fireside Chats

By Jonathan Binkley

Early on a spring evening in the 1930s, our family gathered by a floor-model radio for an evening of listening. Promptly at 7 p.m., a pleasant voice came over the airwaves live from the White House. "My fellow Americans," he said. Or perhaps he would begin with, "My friends … ."

Once again, our 32nd president, Franklin D. Roosevelt, would encourage and persuade us with his effective ability to communicate. Whether by the flourish of his long cigarette holder, the jaunty tilt of his head, the broad, well-toothed smile, or the intonation of his persuasive confidence, he would project confident leadership and personal warmth.

As a "people person," FDR loved nothing better than personally meeting "the folks." His radio fireside chats were just another way to do it. Not only did he become a major American radio personality, but he established an entire list of firsts: first president to broadcast from a foreign country (July 10, 1934 from Cartagena, Colombia); first to broadcast in a foreign language (Nov. 7, 1942, in French to France regarding the war); and first president to appear on television (April 30, 1939, at the New York World's Fair).

Beginning in March 1933 and ending on March 1, 1945, his reassuring voice reached across the airwaves and gave people hope.

From the very start of FDR's public career, his personality was one of his strongest assets. As a New York state senator, governor, assistant secretary of the Navy and presidential candidate, he developed a keen ability to charm all those he met. This charm came across the radio waves, as it seemed to many that he was right there in the room with them.

In the darkest hours of the Great Depression and during the world's greatest war, America needed a confident and reassuring friend. During his fireside chats, FDR shared the voice of friendship. He spoke in a confidential tone as if talking person to person, his voice radiating reassuring support and optimism. By using the radio on a regular basis, FDR rebuilt Americans' confidence in the government. He loved to sermonize, and the public was willing to let him. He explained complicated proposals in simple terms so that all could understand. And FDR used the radio to explain his own actions, too.

Radio was in its infancy when Franklin Roosevelt became the best-known voice in broadcasting. It started in November 1920, when radio was first used for reporting public events, and its influence increased greatly in the following decade. Radio added richness to American life. It drew Americans together in their leisure hours. America was developing a taste for the radio in music, sports, public affairs and entertainment.

The country adjusted well to life by the radio, as did the politicians. By 1928, the radio had become an important vote-getting device. It played a major role when FDR badly beat the luckless Depression president, Herbert Hoover, in 1932.

Of the diversions available during the 1920s and 1930s, none surpassed the radio in popularity. By the end of the 1920s, more than 12 million families had a radio, even though most cost more than $100. With the subsequent arrival of the Great Depression, radio prices fell, and the unemployed had much free time. The convergence of these events saw radios increasing by a third in two years. By the early 1940s, most families would own one.

By March 4, 1933, when FDR took office, the radio was a central fixture in a vast number of American homes. When, in a flurry of action, Roosevelt took strong, immediate measures to get the country moving again, the radio was part of it. To help explain what was happening, FDR took to the radio one week after he was sworn into office. On March 12, 1933, he explained in simple words what had been done and what would be done, and invited all Americans' cooperation.

At 10:30 p.m. that night, facing three microphones in the Oval Office, FDR put out his famous cigarette, took a sip of water and gave birth to one of radio's most famous series. The press promptly labeled them "fireside chats." Roosevelt's personal appeal and homespun simplicity warmed the average citizen. Communication had arrived to fit the times.

Over the next 12 years and three months in office, FDR addressed the nation via radio some 30 times on some of the most momentous decisions and policies of the times. He also called the press around his Oval Office desk for intimate (and often "off the record") press conferences and briefings a total of 998 times.

President Roosevelt addresses the nation via radio.

The press loved these occasions.

Our 33rd president, Harry S. Truman, tried to use the "fireside" format, too. On Jan. 3, 1946, Truman started his out in a familiar way: "Fellow Americans … ." He too urged people to back his legislative programs. Although it was moderately effective and the message very clear, it was too evident that FDR's successor was not like the master communicator he followed.

Years later, President Jimmy Carter would try it. On Feb. 2, 1977, just two weeks after entering office, Carter used radio to explain the need for unity in national goals of government and development. He too borrowed heavily on Roosevelt's approach to this powerful medium.

Later, on March 5, 1977, President Carter tried a radio call-in program during which citizens could talk to the president by phone. More than 9 million Americans tried to call, but only 42 calls reached the Oval Office. It was the nation's first and probably last dial-a-president radio program.

After more than 50 years, FDR's place as a radio icon is secure. He was one of the great radio personalities of the modern era.

One can still imagine a family seated by a floor-model radio, listening intently as a resonant, Eastern-accented radio voice says with confident crispness: "My friends, good evening!" ☆

The Night We Passed the President

By Edna Van Leuven

It was April 1945. My first son was a baby, 7 months old, and we were taking him by train to live in Florida while his father finished training at Buckingham Field close to Fort Myers.

Only a day or two before, our president, Franklin Delano Roosevelt, had died at Warm Springs, Ga. The country was in mourning and the world seemed to stand still, waiting. The man who had led our nation for so many years was gone, and we were numb in the face of this great man's passing.

My husband, our young son and I were leaving from Pennsylvania Station in Philadelphia. The inside of the terminal was like a tomb, quiet despite the many people moving around. Servicemen from all branches were leaving, destined for parts unknown. Many, we all knew, would never return. World War II was far from over.

I can still see the faces of my mother and mother-in-law as our train pulled out of the station. Like everyone in the nation, we had all said too many goodbyes.

Later, after we had settled in our compartment, the conductor knocked on the door. "Pardon me for the interruption," he said, "but I thought you would like to know that this train will pass the one bearing the president's body back from down South. It will happen sometime after we pass through Washington, D.C., and after dark."

Hours later, when the baby had finally gone to sleep, I stepped into the corridor to watch as trains passed us on the other track, lights blinking in quick succession like a flickering movie.

After awhile my husband joined me and we watched through the darkening night. We had no idea just where we were. All that was visible were lights in the houses close to the tracks.

The funeral procession for President Roosevelt in Washington, D.C.

Washington was a long way behind us when we heard another train coming from the opposite direction. It seemed to be moving at a snail's pace. As it began to pass us we could see that the windows were blacked out. There was something about it—the silence, the loneliness of that moment. We both knew.

I could not help myself. Tears flowed down my cheeks and I held my hand over my heart. I looked at my husband. His Air Force uniform was wrinkled from lying next to the son he had met for the first time just weeks before. But he stood proud, somber and erect, lights from the dimly lit corridor glancing off his lieutenant's bars, his hand at a full salute as that blackened train moved past us in the quiet night.

His commander—and our president— was going home. ★

The Suitcase Democrat

By Jack Gallagher

During World War II, I rode on crowded trains more times than I wish to remember, including the troop train in 1946 that took me from San Francisco to the naval base in Sampson, N.Y., where I mustered out of the U.S. Navy. As memorable as that trip was, however, it does not compare with my memory of a much shorter railroad journey of several years earlier.

I was 18 years old, still in training, and my first sea duty was soon to follow. One Saturday morning I boarded a Pennsylvania Railroad coach at Broad Street Station in Philadelphia with my buddy, Bill Eberley, also a naval trainee. We found a seat in the middle of the coach and sat down, ready to travel to Bill's family home, where I looked forward to savoring some of his mother's out-of-this-world homemade ice cream.

On leaving Broad Street Station, I noticed that all seats were occupied and some passengers were standing in the aisles. At the next stop, a lady accompanied by three or four men boarded the train. Because there were no seats available, she sat on her suitcase in the front of the coach. The other members of her party surrounded the lady in such a manner that it was difficult for me to see her. Yet for some reason, my attention remained riveted on that small group as the train resumed its journey.

Shortly thereafter, one of the men moved out of my line of vision, and then I could see the woman's face more clearly. There was no doubt in my mind as to who she was. I nudged Bill.

"That's Mrs. Roosevelt!"

"It sure is!" Bill replied.

"Bill," I said, "this isn't right—two young guys like us having seats and she's sitting on a suitcase."

I was on the aisle side of the seat and Bill was by the window. Thus, I was the logical one to approach her.

"I think I should go up front and offer her our seat, Bill."

"You're right. Go ahead."

I walked up the aisle, but on reaching the group, hesitated to speak directly to her. Nonetheless, I summoned enough courage to talk to one of the men who formed a circle around her.

"Excuse me, but isn't she the president's wife?" I asked.

"Yes, she is," he responded.

"Well, sir, another sailor and I would like to offer her our seat." Before the man could reply, Mrs. Roosevelt looked up at me with a warm, toothy smile. "That's very kind of you and your friend," she said, "but the train will be stopping in Trenton soon, and I'll get a seat there." Then she repeated with genuine sincerity, "But thank you very much."

The press had carried stories about other members of the Roosevelt family taking advantage of their status to obtain preferential treatment during their travels, but Eleanor Roosevelt obviously lived by a higher standard. I was thrilled that she had even talked to me, and sensed that her moral code would not allow her to take a seat from a serviceman in wartime. Nor did she want to call attention to herself.

I returned to my seat and told Bill that Mrs. Roosevelt appreciated our offer, but had declined. When we disembarked in Trenton, we looked through the window of the coach ahead of ours. We could see that she had indeed found a seat and was concentrating on some needle-work she had brought with her.

When Mrs. Eberley served me a large dish of ice cream that evening, I found myself wishing that Mrs. Roosevelt could have shared that magnificent treat with all of us at the Eberley family table. If ever a Democrat was a *democrat*, Eleanor Roosevelt surely was! ☆

Helen Keller in Wrentham

By Alma Andrews as told to her niece, Luciel Cepurneek Wilson

Each summer when I was in high school, Helen Keller came to a large white house on Main Street in Wrentham, Mass., where we lived. She must have been in her early to mid-30s.

Helen Keller and Anne Sullivan would travel on a lecture tour all winter—mostly to colleges—and would make a lot of money. In early summer they would return to Wrentham.

My Aunt Lena did laundry for them at their house and at her own home. A cook, an upstairs maid, a downstairs maid and a gardener were all hired. Jan (pronounced "Yan"), a Latvian from the community, was their chauffeur.

In 1914 I was hired as Miss Keller's companion and personal maid. I was paid $3 a week. I arrived early every morning and made her breakfast. It was always the same; I would take one fresh egg, separate it and beat the white stiff. Then I would beat the yoke fluffy in a separate bowl. Into this bowl I would mix a glass of freshly squeezed orange juice. Finally, I would fold in the egg white and pour it all into a special bowl to a certain line. Miss Keller ate this mixture with a spoon.

After breakfast I had to clean her room and study. There was little to do—a bit of dusting, straightening up and using a carpet sweeper once in a while. The rooms were very sparsely furnished. No one else cleaned Miss Keller's room, and the other maids weren't allowed in. I had to put everything back exactly so Miss Keller could find things.

I don't remember what she had for lunch, but it was always the same and not enough to keep a bird alive. She ate lunch alone. After making her lunch and serving it, I ate in the kitchen with Jan.

In the afternoon, Miss Keller walked with Professor White, who gave her voice lessons, or she walked in the garden. She could go outside alone. She knew her way, but she always said she could go faster if "Miss Dimples"—that's what she called me—went with her. Miss Keller would pick lettuce and tend the long-stemmed roses in the yard.

Later in the afternoon, I would make a batch of mayonnaise from scratch. At teatime Miss Keller would have sandwiches of garden lettuce and mayonnaise. The bread had been freshly baked by Jan, who sliced it the thinnest I ever saw—like paper. I left for home after tea.

All the others in the house were known as "them." Professor White, Anne Sullivan, Mrs. Tyson (Helen Keller's married sister) and Mrs. Tyson's little daughter stayed there all summer. Miss Keller had dinner with "them" every night.

On stormy days and sometimes in the mornings, Miss Keller and the professor walked up and down the big porch of the Wrentham house. We could hear them as they did their exercises— "Ahhh, eee, ohhh …" and so forth. In the afternoons they walked around town, continuing their drills as they went.

Often they walked along Thurston Street, which was diagonal to Main Street, and many times they stopped at my house. My father raised huge white rabbits for food. Miss Keller liked to go up to the barn to hold and pet the rabbits.

My brother, Fred, was 10 or 12, and Miss Keller would feel all over his face with her fingertips to see who he was. He stood there politely for as long as he had to. Sometimes Miss Keller would sit under our grape arbor to get out of the sun. Mother shared flowers but didn't converse with Miss Keller. Mother didn't speak much English.

I didn't like Anne Sullivan. She was very cold and often rude, both to Miss Keller and to others. Once unexpected company came in the afternoon, upsetting the usual routine. Mrs. Tyson called me and asked me to take her daughter for a walk. Miss Sullivan got mad and yelled at her, saying that I wasn't hired to be a baby sitter. She always criticized Miss Keller, too; she was very, very odd.

There were always visitors; they entertained a lot during the summer. Miss Sullivan served as the hostess. They ran up large bills at the local butcher's and at Thomas' market.

By the end of the summer, the money from the lectures would run out and the servants would be let go one by one. I was the first to go both summers I worked for them. Those who were left took on more jobs until only Jan was left. In the end, he was cook, maid, handyman and chauffeur, and he even washed the ladies' hair.

Mrs. Tyson went back to Alabama, and by October the house would be closed. Miss Keller and Miss Sullivan would go back on the road on their lecture tour. I think Jan went with them as chauffeur.

They had a large car. One day in 1912 or 1913, Jan drove into my father's yard in a large, fancy touring car. I don't think he had ever driven a motorcar before that day; he was weaving all over the road. He told my mother

Helen Keller and Anne Sullivan, circa 1914. Photo courtesy Perkins School for the Blind, Watertown, Mass.

that he wanted to give me my first ride, but my mother was scared and refused.

But my father was interested in the car. When Jan invited him to go, I went with them and sat in the back. Jan explained everything to my father as we wove up the street. In turning around we almost hit a tree and a stone wall. When we returned, my mother was surprised to see us alive.

I don't remember Miss Keller ever riding around town in the car, though. Jan used it mostly for errands during the summer.

In 1915 I graduated from Wrentham High School. Several girls in the class received bouquets from the florist in Franklin, but I knew my family couldn't afford that, so I didn't expect any.

Then, on the day of my graduation, Miss Keller's car pulled up in the front yard. Jan had a gift from Miss Keller. It was a book of Shakespeare, signed by Miss Keller, in which she had written a verse for me. On top of the book were six long-stemmed roses that Miss Keller had picked. She was always so thoughtful.

At the end of the summer in 1915, I got a full-time job in Boston. I never worked for Miss Keller again. I think Miss Keller's house was purchased and converted into a rest home; I believe it's still there, about a mile out of town.

To many people, Helen Keller was a heroine. To me she would be that and more. She was one of the nicest people I ever met. ✪

America's Cowboy Philosopher

By Henry J. Pratt

Everybody liked Will Rogers, and today, more than six decades after his death in a plane crash in Alaska, national interest in the Western cracker-barrel philosopher is rekindled. The Broadway hit *The Will Rogers Follies* won six Tony awards and in 1991 was named the season's best Broadway play by Drama Desk, a critics group. CBS-Fox Home Videotapes of four Rogers films, including many silent slapsticks and 21 in sound, are popular.

In many ways, Will Rogers—perhaps the greatest and most loquacious cowboy-humorist ever—is well and fondly remembered. Regally nestled on a hilltop over-looking his beloved Claremore, Okla., the Will Rogers Memorial frames the family tomb and museum. Over the years, millions have visited the 20-acre site.

Memorial director Joe Carter has written *Never Met a Man I Didn't Like*, a book that includes a Rogers biography and some of his most memorable quotations. "Much of Rogers' timeless allure is in his political relevance," Carter explains. The cowboy-raised trick roper, movie and vaudeville star, newspaper columnist,

radio commentator and adventurer loved to poke fun at policticians' follies.

In explaining the Western humorist's come-back, Carter says, "He articulated an agrarian populist view, was able to reduce complexities to understandable terms, and meshed these complicated ideas with everyday humor." Men and women everywhere labeled Rogers an "ambassador of goodwill" and "congressman-at-large."

Rogers claimed, "I'm not a member of any organized party. I'm a Democrat." He once suggested, "This year is TYFOH: Tough Year for Office Holders."

Tabbed in the late 1920s as "the nation's conscience," Rogers once quipped that "America's diplomacy is an open book—a checkbook." He also re-marked, "I never met a man I didn't like," and, "We are the first nation in the history of the world to go to the poorhouse in an automobile."

Will Rogers was born William Penn Adair Rogers was on Nov. 4, 1879, on his family's ranch near Oologah, in the Indian Territory of Oklahoma. ("Nobody but an Indian can pronounce Oologah," Will Rogers used to say.) Close to Claremore, the Will Rogers

The White House on the Verdigris, Will Rogers' birthplace. This home was built in the years following the Civil War. By 1879, when Will was born, the second story and white siding had been added. The Will Rogers Memorial Commission has carefully restored the home to conditions of those Indian Territory days. Photo courtesy Will Rogers Memorial Museum.

birthplace was later moved about a half-mile from its original site to make way for the Oologah Lake Dam.

The Rogers home was often a gathering place for Cherokee Nation leaders and was referred to as "the White House on the Verdigris." One of the finest homes in Indian country, it was completed by Clem Vann Rogers in 1875. He and his wife, Mary America, both one quarter Cherokee, worked diligently to expand their cattle ranch to nearly 60,000 acres.

In these surroundings, the couple's eighth child—and only son to grow to adulthood—was born. The parlor of Clem and Mary Rogers' home today remains as it was then. A portrait of Will as a baby hangs over a crib, and period furnishings fill the house, which is open to the public.

As a youngster, Will enjoyed wearing Western clothes, riding ponies and practicing lariat tricks. His cattle baron dad gave Will his first pony when he was 5 years old, and at age 9 he took part in his first roundup.

When Will later showed up at Kemper Military School in Boonville, Mo., he brought with him lariats of various sizes, a cowboy hat, a flannel shirt with a fiery red bandanna, a brightly colored vest, high-heeled, red-topped boots and spurs. The teen-age cowboy liked Kemper at first, getting his best grades in American history and elocution; but he got lower grades in other subjects.

During his two years at Kemper, he displayed a remarkable memory and frequently astounded classmates with his gift of gab. Will

Will Rogers began doing vaudeville acts with his highly-skilled lariat trick roping in 1905. All that culminated in his first appearance in The Ziegfeld Follies of 1916. *Photo courtesy Rogers Memorial Museum.*

was proud of his Cherokee blood, and often noted for others that his people had met—not sailed on—the Mayflower.

When he turned 18, Will quit the classroom and hit the trail of life. Following stints working in South America and South Africa, Rogers in 1903 joined an outfit called Texas Jack's Wild West Show. Billed as "The Cherokee Kid," he performed a trick-roping number.

Rogers began doing pokey-patter between and during his rope tricks. When he found that he had a rare gift for chiding others and poking fun without drawing blood, his show-biz career expanded.

In 1905 Will began the vaudeville chapter in his diversified career, which culminated in his first appearance in *The Ziegfeld Follies of 1916*. Fame came fast and furious, catapulting Rogers into movies in 1919. Surprisingly, for someone whose humor was primarily verbal, Rogers did especially well in silent parodies.

In 1929 Will was signed by Fox Studios. He spent the rest of his life doing up to three sound pictures a year. All of Rogers' pictures were fairly inexpensive, and each was declared successful. But only two of them, *Steamboat Round the Bend* and *Judge Priest*, both directed by John Ford, are particularly distinguished.

Rogers also kept his typewriter humming merrily. His highly popular newspaper column, only a few paragraphs long, was usually printed in a box under the title "Will Rogers Says." Appearing in more than 400 papers across the nation, it was easily the most widely read column of the era.

Rogers wrote more than 665 weekly articles and did 69 radio broadcasts. He wrote for *The Saturday Evening Post, Life* and other magazines. He wrote and had published more than 2 million words in his lifetime, equal to some 20 novels. All that helped the ex-cowpoke earn about $20,000 weekly.

Concerning the United States presidency, millions loved this Rogers gem: "It's not a disgrace not to be able to run a country nowadays, but it is a disgrace to keep on trying when you can't." He also quipped: "There's only one amusement line I've not yet tried, and that's to go to the U.S. Senate."

Will married the former Betty Blake after a long courtship conducted largely by mail. She became a tour companion, a helpful advisor and ardent biographer. The couple had four children: Will Jr., Mary, Jim and Fred.

Will Rogers awaits an aerial takeoff in 1927. From the Collections of Henry Ford Museum & Greenfield Village.

On their last fateful airplane trip together, noted aviator and fellow Oklahoman Wiley Post met Rogers in Seattle, and the duo enjoyed perfect flying weather up the Canadian coast to Alaska. Fifty miles out of Fairbanks, Post and Rogers landed at a river mouth to check their flight course with Eskimo seal hunters.

The Eskimos then watched the little red plane with its oversized pontoons lift slowly, bank, then nose upward through the fog. But then the plane fell, crumpled on the earth, and settled on its back, killing Post and the 55-year-old Rogers instantly. After a brief and eerie silence in the snow, the Eskimos cried for help and sped to a nearby village to report the incident.

News of the crash on Aug. 15, 1935, stunned the world. One of Will's greatest admirers, President Franklin D. Roosevelt, said, "There was something infectious about his humor. Above all things, in a time grown too solemn and somber, he brought his countrymen back to a sense of proportion."

Rogers' Santa Monica home with all its treasures is a California State Park. Overlooking Colorado Springs, Colo., high on Cheyenne Mountain, is the Will Rogers Shrine of the Sun, where the chimes ring every quarter-hour in his memory. They chime to help honor the Western cowboy-turned-philosopher whose spirit and influence on America lives on for the ages.

In the U.S. Capitol's Statuary Hall in Washington, D.C., stands a large bronze statue of Rogers, slouched in his familiar way with hands thrust deep into his pockets. His warm and gentle eyes look down upon members of Congress who were so often the targets of his remarks and whom he once called "our hired help."

Biographer Shannon Garst, in her moving book *Will Rogers, Immortal Cowboy*, concludes, "Will's spirit is enshrined in the hearts of his countrymen as one of their great folk heroes." Though Will Rogers was born on a cattle ranch in Indian Territory as a common man, he had a delightfully uncommon touch and was right for America—not only in his day but also for all seasons. ☆

The Rough Rider

By Orvil M. James

The date was May 20, 1903. President Theodore Roosevelt was on the campaign trail, and his train had whistle-stopped briefly on a siding at Edgewood in Northern California to allow the southbound train to pass.

The snow-crowned peak of Mount Shasta provided a perfect backdrop for the scene as President Roosevelt spoke briefly from the rear platform of the train to a handful of citizens who were on hand to greet him.

I was only 4 years old, but this memorable occasion is firmly implanted in my mind due to the president's dynamic personality and the scenic beauty of the spot at which the meeting occurred.

As Roosevelt began to speak, I pushed forward eagerly to get a closer look at the great man who had led his Rough Riders in their famous charge up San Juan Hill. Being the only small child present, I must have attracted his attention. Before I realized what was happening, I was being handed up onto the platform to shake hands with the president.

I distinctly remember the tweedy suit he was wearing, the eyeglasses, and his toothy smile. His friendly, fatherly manner made a deep impression on me and I liked him instantly.

Afterward, standing near the tracks of the departing train, I was reluctant to leave. With several of his campaign cards in my hands, I watched his train as it left a trail of smoke and steam behind and receded into the distance behind the 14,161-foot snow-clad peak of Mount Shasta.

It was a great moment in my life, one to be treasured in memory throughout the years. I cannot help but think, *Here, indeed, was a man to match our mountains.* ✯

The original Rough Rider, Theodore Roosevelt.

Lucky Lindy

By Martin Cole

*M*onday, Feb. 20, 1928, was freezing cold, with penetrating icy blasts sweeping across Peoria's Big Hollow Airport. I should know. I was there.

Ten thousand people were there that last afternoon. Held in check by companies of the National Guard, they milled around and stamped their feet to keep the blood circulating.

All were there with a single-minded purpose. They had come to see the world's greatest hero. No one other than Charles Lindbergh could draw such a crowd on a day hardly fit for man or beast.

Lindbergh was not due until 6 o'clock, but most of the crowd—Peorians, farmers and townspeople from surrounding communities, along with Jay Bowman and I, who had hitchhiked from Toulon—had come early. And so, for an hour or so, we too shivered and stamped our feet as the feeble sun sank toward the horizon and stars began to appear in the gathering dusk.

Lindy proudly poses in front of his airplane in 1927. From the Collections of Henry Ford Museum and Greenfield Village.

The occasion for Lindbergh's visit was a commemorative airmail flight. During the preceding year he had flown the mail between St. Louis, Springfield, Peoria and Chicago in weather fair and foul, all the while dreaming of making a nonstop flight from New York to Paris. To make a long and heroic story short, he took a leave of absence, got some backing and sank his savings into a monoplane. While the world held its collective breath for 33½ hours, he crossed a stormy Atlantic to reach Le Bourget Field, Paris. The world went wild!

At the height of this adulation, Lindbergh, as modest and shy as ever, was induced to fly a commemorative airmail schedule. So, on Feb. 20, he would again fly across familiar Illinois cornfields from St. Louis to Chicago, and on the following day make a return flight.

It was assumed that there would be several planeloads of commemorative letters and postcards bearing the special cancellation "Lindbergh Again Flies the Airmail." To carry the overloads, additional planes flown by airmail buddies would accompany Lindbergh. Yet, in keeping the promise that Lindbergh would personally fly each piece of mail during a portion of the route, his red Travelair plane was unloaded at each stop and the mail shifted to one of the accompanying Douglas 02 planes. It was this arrangement that brought about the small incident I remembered.

Six o'clock skipped by. Lindbergh was late. A curtain of darkness settled over Big Hollow Airport. Our eyes adjusted to the darkness, aided somewhat by occasional car lights and blobs of runway lights giving off faint illumination. As the minutes dragged on, we hunched to get as much protection as possible from upturned sheepskin collars, stamped our feet and shivered. But no one left.

Before darkness closed in, I observed the gasoline truck parked on the opposite side of the field. I thought little of this until I saw the mail trucks crossing the runway and heading that direction. When I mentioned it to Jay, we both told ourselves that Lindbergh would likely taxi directly to the trucks.

"Well, I wonder if it's worthwhile to stick around?" There was a note of disappointment in Jay's voice. I guess he was thinking what I was thinking: We had hitchhiked 40 miles for nothing. It looked like a lot of people would be disappointed. I probably wouldn't be as disappointed as some, because I had seen Lindbergh before, back when he was just another airmail pilot. My father and I had been returning from Peoria in the family Dodge, and when we saw the evening mail plane arriving, we hastily wheeled the car into the airport. (Airplanes then were an uncommon sight, and the miracle of flight never ceased to amaze us.)

The DH-4 was piloted by a tall, boyish pilot who seemed too young for so important a mission. His youth made an impression on me, and the image lingered. When that same smiling, boyish image became familiar to everyone, I was able to say, "Lindbergh—sure, I remember him."

I don't know who thought of it first, but when Jay said, "Let's go," we were borrowing from an ancient proverb: If Lindbergh couldn't come to us, we would go to Lindbergh.

To reach the opposite side of the runway, we had to jog a quarter-mile to Dunlap Road, where the airport began, and cross there. Try running at night over strange ground while dressed in bulky winter clothing and wearing four-buckle overshoes. But with time against us, we hardly dared slacken our pace.

We were making the crossover when the planes arrived. They whizzed over our heads—rather close, it seemed—and landed on the frozen sod beyond. And as we guessed, they taxied directly to the lights where the trucks were parked. By the time Jay and I arrived somewhat out of breath, we had missed the official welcome. The newspapers would say that Lindbergh had cut short the welcoming speeches to get on with the handling of mail.

Within the glare of headlights were some 30 or 40 persons. Some were gassing Lindbergh's red Travelair and the four accompanying Douglas 02's. Others were handling mail. Maybe a dozen or so city and mail officials and

several reporters were attempting conversation with a busy Lindbergh, who was bundled in a teddy-bear flying suit and sheepskin boots.

Again I was struck by Lindbergh's youthfulness. He seemed to exemplify the storybook all-American boy who prevails over all odds. But tonight, Lindbergh was in a rush; he hurried, and didn't prolong any conversation. He didn't say as much but I guessed he was anxious to make up some lost time.

Then one official had a brilliant idea, or so he must have thought. "Colonel," he said to Lindbergh, "it's late. No one will know differently if you go ahead and let us send the mail in another plane."

I was dumbfounded. *No one will know differently … .* Well, *I* would know. And why wouldn't I tell my friends in Toulon? There were 300 letters from Toulon in those sacks! And I had a postcard in one of them—a picture of Lindbergh standing beside the Spirit of St. Louis! The cards had been sold for the occasion by the Peoria American Legion.

Lindbergh was bending over a mail sack when the official made his offensive suggestion. It was a moment of crisis for me; if Lindbergh didn't carry the Peoria mail, his hero image would vanish as far as I was concerned. And perhaps just as important, my faith in mankind would be severely jolted.

I needn't have worried. Lindbergh's answer came instantly. He straightened up and replied in a voice that was surprisingly soft, yet his tone left little doubt that he was shocked by the suggestion. "People expect me to carry the mail," he said evenly. "I will carry it." And that was that.

And so the Travelair was emptied of mail sacks and the Peoria mail was stowed aboard. Then Lindbergh did something that endeared him to me more than ever. He showed himself to the 10,000 who had waited, some for two hours, in the bitter cold. He stood apart on the runway with headlights turned on him. He waved. The crowd cheered; they would go home thrilled and satisfied.

Jay and I returned to Toulon. And of course, we had to tell just about everyone in the town's population of 1,200 how we stood beside Lindbergh during a moment of decision.

"Yeah, we stood right beside him … ." ☆

I Knew Carry A. Nation

By Lola Mae Jackson

I grew up in Guthrie, Okla., and Carry Nation lived just across the alley from us, in a large white house with a barn in the rear. The carriage and two horses she stabled in the barn took her over practically all of Oklahoma and Kansas, where she lectured on the evils of alcohol and tobacco.

Carry Amelia Moore was born in Garrard County, Ky., on November 25, 1846, and her family moved frequently from place to place in Kentucky, Missouri and Texas. While quite young, she married a young physician who died of alcoholism soon thereafter.

After several years as a primary schoolteacher in Holden, Mo., she married David Nation, a minister and lawyer. As she began spending more time away from home on her temperance campaigns, her husband gave her an ultimatum: give up her crusade against liquor or he would divorce her. She chose to stay with what she believed to be her calling. Carry continued to use her name, Carry A. Nation, as a providential symbol of her divine calling, although some erroneously printed her name as "Carrie" (as in the poster at right). It would become her life's work to "carry a nation."

She came to Guthrie in 1904 or 1905 and with a small printing press, she established *The Hatchet,* a publication to fight alcohol, freemasonry and republicanism. Carry believed that because of the fundamentalist religion that was prevalent in Oklahoma, the state constitution would include a liquor-prohibition clause. However, so long as Oklahoma remained in the hands of the federal government, saloons and liquor by the drink would be legal.

While living in Guthrie, she started her temperance magazine, *The Hatchet,* in an attempt to strike at the root of the liquor traffic through politics seeking a constitutional prohibition.

Wielding a hatchet, she entered taverns and saloons, breaking bottles of liquor and the large mirrors that often hung behind the bars. Sometimes she even chopped up some of the furniture, including the actual bars and back bars. She had small, gold, hatchet-shaped pins made and sold them or gave them away as souvenirs.

I remember one Saturday evening when she swept into the largest saloon in Guthrie, probably at its busiest hour. She broke every bottle on the bar and on the back bar. She also smashed the large mirror over the back bar before she launched into a spirited lecture on the evils of alcohol. Then she simply walked out, leaving the spectators—including the owner—speechless.

She was not always permitted to work unimpeded. Several times she was arrested and jailed for destroying property. On those occasions, she paid her fine and then went right on with her crusade.

One night her barn caught fire. My brother, who was about 12 years old, had been helping Mrs. Nation take care of her horses and carriage equipment. He jumped out of bed and ran to see about the horses. They were taken out safely but the carriage was damaged. Many townspeople suspected that the fire had been set by someone who resented her interference in their drinking, or who had suffered property destruction at her hands.

Carry left Guthrie to live in Washington, D.C., where she continued to publish *The Hatchet* and fight for Prohibition. She later returned to the Southwest and died in Leavenworth, Kan., on June 9, 1911. She is buried in Belton, Mo. ✮

America's Quiet Hero

By Lina Accurso

Sgt. Alvin C. York in military uniform during World War I. This photo and accompanying photos in this story courtesy Tennessee Department of Environment & Conservation and the York family.

Editor's note: In 1993, my wife, Janice, and I began a nationwide campaign to convince the U.S. Postal Service to honor Sgt. Alvin York with a postage stamp. Lina Accurso's article below, which I published in the November 1993 issue of Good Old Days magazine was the genesis of that effort. When the "Distinguished Soldiers" set of postage stamps issued by the U.S. Postal Service was released in May 2000, Sgt. Alvin York was one of four American war heroes featured. The others were John Hines from World War I, and World War II veterans Omar Bradley and Audie Murphy. Janice and I are proud to have helped honor this great, but quiet, American hero.—Ken Tate, Editor

I'm as big an Elvis fan as anyone. But I am annoyed that he got a stamp while my one-woman campaign to get a stamp in time for the 100th birthday of one of my heroes failed.

Alvin Cullum York was born on Dec. 13, 1887, in Pall Mall, in the Valley of the Three Forks of the Wolf in Tennessee. He deserves to be remembered and thanked by all Americans.

Best known as Sgt. York, he was the most famous hero of World War I. He single-handedly captured 132 German soldiers, killed another 25, and silenced 35 machine guns.

This feat, performed in less than four hours during the Battle of the Argonne Forest on Oct. 8, 1918, is still the biggest one-man catch in recorded military history. And York didn't do it with Rambo-style automatic weapons. He did it with one rifle and, when that ran out of bullets, a pistol.

York's solo victory so disheartened Germany that it was cited as one of the factors in the Armistice one month later, on Nov. 11, 1918. Gen. Pershing called York "the greatest civilian soldier of the war." France's Marshal Foch said, "What you did was the greatest thing accomplished by any private soldier of all the armies in Europe."

York's performance earned him a promotion from corporal to sergeant, and he received more than 50 medals from France, England, Italy and the United States, including our highest award, the Congressional Medal of Honor. When he returned to the United States in triumph, the stock market gave him a standing ovation, as did Congress.

Unfortunately, today his name is also linked to an ill-conceived 1981 defensive weaponry system that was obsolete as soon as it was built. The system was named in his honor, but at a cost of $1.8 billion, *that* "Sergeant York" became an example of Pentagon waste.

Better to disregard that ill-begotten gun and remember him as he was portrayed in the 1941 movie *Sergeant York*, for which Gary Cooper won his first Oscar. It is still my all-time favorite movie. The film adhered closely to the facts of York's life, and it often runs on television during religious and patriotic holidays.

However, even this great film must have been a mixed blessing for York: It remembers him for the day that he least liked to remember. A religious man, he originally had requested exemption from military service as a conscientious objector but his request was denied.

York was born into poverty, one of 11 children of a hardworking father and a deeply religious mother. He had a third-grade education. When his father, William, died in 1911, he helped work the family farm and blacksmith shop.

He took any job he could get, including one at a lumber camp. There he picked up a distressing talent for smoking, card playing, drinking and barroom brawling.

That York did not end up as just another ne'er-do-well was due, he later said, to the intervention of "God and Miss Gracie."

York was drinking with his friends at a town get-together when he saw a teen-age girl he had known since she was a baby. He was 12 years older than she was, but once he saw the grown-up Gracie Williams, he never drank, fought, smoked, swore or gambled again.

He later explained, "Miss Gracie wouldn't let me come a-courting until I quit my mean drinking, fighting and card-flipping. I was struck down with the power of love and the great God Almighty all together."

792 Sgt. Alvin York, from a photograph in the United States Signal Corps, War Department, Washington.

Gracie was very religious, so besides changing his habits, York joined her church, later becoming a second elder. He sang in the choir, read the Bible from cover to cover and taught Sunday school. His life now in order, he had everything to live for—and then he received a notice from his draft board.

York despised killing. He didn't understand the war and did his best not to go. His appeals were rejected, however, and he had to go anyway.

He kept a diary in a small red memorandum book and wrote about his early days in Camp Gordon, Ga.

"Those were trying hours for a boy like me, trying to live for God and do His blessed will … . Then the Lord would give me help to bear my hard tasks. So there I was, the homesickest boy you ever saw."

But York's spirits revived at target practice. Back in Tennessee, he'd been the best shot for miles around. He had even shot his initials into trees while riding on his donkey, stone drunk.

Stone sober, he was even better. To the delight of his officers, he happily blasted target after target to pieces. But he balked when they put up a human silhouette. "Sir, I'm doing wrong. Practicing to kill people is against my religion," he said.

York was brought to the camp commander. They debated the Bible for three days, with the uneducated York fighting the officer to a draw. The commander allowed York to go back to Tennessee to think things over, promising him the longed-for exemption if he still could not reconcile himself to the necessity of the war.

York took his Bible to a hilltop and sat there for two full days.

He never fully explained why he decided to return. But his marksmanship won him the rank of corporal, and he was sent to France. He and his company ended up in the Argonne in northeastern France, just south of Belgium, where the Germans had set up their nearly unbreakable Hindenburg Line.

It was there, during a battle that began at exactly 6:10 a.m. on Oct. 8, 1918, that the conscientious objector became a war hero.

When York was later asked by his superiors how he had conquered so many Germans by himself, he simply said, "I surrounded 'em." The full details were recounted by the Americans who had been with him, as well as the Germans he took prisoner.

They told how a small detachment including York was sent behind a hill where the Germans were firing from a high ridge covered with trees and bushes. The Americans had captured about 30 of the enemy on the ground when the German machine gunners quietly turned around, motioned to their captured comrades to hit the ground and fired directly into the Americans. Many were killed or injured.

Though only a lowly corporal, York was the highest-ranking officer left unhurt. Ordering the eight remaining uninjured Americans to guard the Germans, York stormed the ridge by himself as bullets churned up the ground around him. He fired so quickly that many Germans instantly surrendered, thinking the woods were filled with American marksmen. The remaining Germans formed a line on the hill where they charged the lone American—and lost.

When all the Germans gave up, York and his troops (all eight of them) marched the Germans for miles back to the American camp. At one point they were lost, and York asked a German captain which way to go. When the officer pointed one way, York shrewdly marched them in the opposite direction.

After depositing his 132 prisoners he told the commanding officer, "Ready for duty, Sir." It was 10 a.m.; to him, it had been just half a morning's work.

He told the *Saturday Evening Post*, in the April 1919 article that cemented his fame, that he was proud of the fact that throughout the entire inferno, he hadn't uttered "a single cuss."

Though York may have sounded charmingly blasé to his officers and the press, the notes he wrote in his little red diary the day after the battle betray far more tormented thoughts. He and the remnant of his battle-torn company went back to the battlefield to find and bury their slain comrades.

York wrote: "Everything destroyed, torn up, killed. Trees, grass, men. We yelled, thinking that maybe somebody was in the bushes, but nobody yelled back … .

"Corporal Murray Savage, my best pal, dead. I was mussed up inside worser than I ever been. I didn't want to kill a whole heap of Germans no how. I didn't hate them. But I done it just the same. I have tried to forget."

But the world did not let York forget. On his return to America he was flooded with offers for movies, endorsements, and the Ziegfeld Follies. He refused them all.

Three weeks after setting foot back in the states, he and Gracie were married by the governor of Tennessee on the rock ledge where they once had met. Two thousand people attended the ceremony. The newlyweds moved into a farmhouse given to them by the people of Tennessee, built on land his ancestors had once owned but had been forced to sell.

York rarely showed off his medals or spoke of his war experiences. But he did set up a foundation that would provide education for poor children of the region. He threw himself into his church, his charities and his family, since he and Gracie had seven children.

He tried to avoid the limelight, always saying, "Uncle Sam's uniform ain't for sale." He rejected offers to sell his story, even during the Depression when he—like other farmers—was in danger of losing his farm and home.

York had refused Hollywood producer Jesse Lasky several times over the years, the first time in 1919, right after Lasky attended the New York City ticker-tape parade held immediately after York's return.

But in 1940, Lasky decided to try once more. This time, he had the one argument that could sway York: America once again seemed headed toward war in Europe, and it was York's patriotic duty to inspire frightened troops. And so, 21 years after the subject was first broached, York finally agreed.

However, the uneducated Tennessee farmer didn't let the big Hollywood producer off the hook easily. He made him agree in writing—with Tennessee Gov. Prentice Cooper as witness—to certain conditions.

The film had to be accurate. Though York wouldn't take any money personally, his royalties had to be used to set up a Bible school. No actress who smoked, drank or was any kind of "oomph girl" could play Gracie. And the actor who played him had to be the only actor he liked: Gary Cooper.

At least one of Cooper's biographers suggested that Cooper was Lasky's idea all along, that Lasky maneuvered York into asking for Cooper, even going so far as to send Cooper a telegram in York's name. However, it seems unlikely that Lasky would alienate York at that late date by lying and forging his name.

That theory also assumes that York could be manipulated. Uneducated he may have been, but he had never been anybody's patsy; 132 Germans had learned that the hard way.

But when Lasky asked Cooper, the star refused outright. He openly admitted to being scared: "Sgt. York was too big for me. He covered too much territory."

The Yorks' Wolf Creek home in Tennessee.

Henry Fonda and James Stewart had none of Cooper's qualms about taking the role and were, in fact, closer to York's age at the time of the events depicted than the 39-year-old Cooper. But York would have Cooper or no one, so Lasky told Cooper that it was *his* patriotic duty to do it.

When Cooper traveled to Tennessee to meet York, York gave him a 125-year-old muzzle gun. Cooper was a crack shot and he and York talked guns for hours. And when Cooper returned to California, he returned as the man who would play Sgt. York.

Attention turned to the casting of Gracie. York's conditions were so hard to meet in Hollywood that Joan Leslie, a girl who would turn 16 during filming, was cast. Leslie had worked well with older men in films; she'd appeared in *High Sierra* with Humphrey Bogart

the year before and in *Yankee Doodle Dandy* with James Cagney the year after. Moreover, Gracie had been Leslie's age during the events of the film.

Nevertheless, Cooper muttered that he felt like a criminal every time he kissed the underage girl. And he was so nervous about attempting to duplicate the war hero's accent that the usually affable Cooper was agitated throughout the filming.

He needn't have been. The role became one of his favorites among 92 leading roles. It was definitely his parents' favorite; York stayed with them when he visited during the film's shooting.

Sergeant York was filled with real, lovable people, and Cooper's uneducated, hot-tempered York, struggling with his conscience at every turn, is the most real and lovable of them all.

Sergeant York was one of the screen's first attempts to realistically portray poverty and the hardships of farmers, and to treat the rural people in the film with respect instead of stereotyping them as bumpkins and hillbillies.

Because of York's insistence that the film stick to the facts, the movie stands head and shoulders above the usual stylized Hollywood biographies.

Naturally, events had to be condensed for time's sake. The three-day debate between York and his officers runs 6 minutes; York's two-day struggle over whether to return to the Army takes 3 minutes. York killed 25 German soldiers in only 3 minutes, and the entire battle takes less than 10 minutes to complete.

When Cooper, as York, enters the battle, *Yankee Doodle* plays underneath. But after that there is no music. There are only the sounds of bombs and bullets and men groaning as they fall. There was no blood lust in York, and there is none in his movie.

Sergeant York was released in July 1941. Pearl Harbor was bombed in December. When Cooper was awarded the Oscar the following February, America had been at war for two months. The film helped America face its terrible moral dilemma not with rage, but with faith.

In receiving his Oscar, Cooper said, "Gary Cooper didn't win this award. It was Sgt. York, because to the best of my ability, I tried to *be* Sgt. York." For the rest of his life, Cooper credited York for his first Oscar.

Perhaps most inspiring was that in the 23 years between World War I and the film's release, York remained an untarnished hero. He was untainted by ego, greed or scandal. He'd gone back to his hometown and his sweetheart, and lived a quiet life of faith and work. If *he* could come through the fire unscarred physically and spiritually, perhaps America could, too.

But peacetime would be harder on York. True to his word, he had donated all of the almost $200,000 he received from the film to his Bible school. However, the Internal Revenue Service ruled that the money was personal income. In 1951, the IRS hit him with fines, back taxes and interest totaling $172,000.

Threatened with the loss of his farm and his home, York was most deeply hurt by the notion that his country now accused him of cheating. He said bitterly, "I paid 'em what I owed 'em," and fought the IRS for 10 years. When Sam Rayburn, Speaker of the House of Representatives, heard

Alvin York with "Miss Gracie" on the lawn of their Wolf Creek, Tenn., home.

of York's plight, he began a public fund-raising drive to pay off the tax.

Stung by the bad publicity the case engendered, the IRS settled for the $25,000 that Rayburn had raised to that point.

But York's problems were far from over. In 1954, a stroke put him in a wheelchair for the rest of his life. Gracie tended him devotedly. But his illness and IRS problems, plus his chronic over-generosity, drained his limited income from the farm. The Dupont family of Delaware set up a trust fund that gave him $300 a month for the rest of his life. He died on Sept. 2, 1964.

In its Sept. 11 issue, *Time* reported York's death under the title "One Day's Work." The article said that everything in York's life after the morning of Oct. 8, 1918, was "anticlimactic."

From the world's point of view, that may be a correct assessment. But it isn't my view, and I don't think it was York's. When he returned to Tennessee after the war, neighbors saw him sit silently for hours at night, staring into the hills.

When asked what he was thinking about as he killed Germans, he gave no speeches about heroism or even patriotic duty. Instead, he said that as he fired, he prayed for forgiveness for killing; he prayed for the souls of the men he was forced to kill; and he prayed that they'd surrender quickly so he wouldn't have to kill any more of them.

What Alvin York *thought* that day was even more important than what he *did.* And the peaceful and honorable conduct of the rest of his long life was even nobler than what he did during those four momentous hours of it.

Now, in a new century, Alvin York deserves to be remembered and honored just as much as he was then. ☆

What We Did Back Home

By Jean Powis

Although fighting Americans "over there" kept our country safe during World War II, the folks on the home front—embracing the theme "I will work, sacrifice and endure"—should also be remembered for the part they played in supporting our Armed Forces.

That was a dreadful day back in December 1941, when President Franklin Roosevelt took to the radio to announce to more than 60 million Americans that the Japanese had bombed Pearl Harbor. Newspaper carriers crowded the streets shouting, "Extra! Extra! Japan attacks Pearl Harbor!" Terrified citizens knew that the United States was going to war.

Immediately following our entry into the war, the military services were swamped with patriotic male and female volunteers. An even greater number of male draftees reported for duty, leaving many jobs and other tasks on the home front to the women of the country.

Apprehensive but determined to help America, women virtually took over factory jobs that once had been handled solely by men. In the process, they proved that they could do those jobs just as well as—and in some cases *better* than—the men they had replaced.

One of the most widely recognized jobs in defense plants was that of the riveters who assembled airplanes. Trading in their dresses for slacks, their heads covered with scarves, women worked in pairs as they riveted their way into aviation production.

Out of this patriotic effort was born "Rosie the Riveter," the mythical defense-worker heroine of World War II. She was celebrated on magazine covers and posters, in film and song, and she was a great recruiting tool to draw women into wartime manufacturing.

Labor shortages resulting from the military's demand for men left women to become not only riveters but welders, mechanics, crane operators, truck drivers, gas-station attendants and professionals as well. At the same time, women continued to cook, clean, shop and care for their children.

Besides filling many paid positions to aid the war effort, many women freely volunteered to work in the United Services Organization (USO), the Red Cross, and as civil-defense wardens, ambulance drivers and firefighters.

Keeping up GI morale was another task assigned to American women. Their personal correspondence with servicemen proved to be a valuable asset in the psychological side of the war. While their letters provided our fighting men with hometown news, they also assured them that their loved ones missed them, but that they were in good health and out of danger.

Hollywood played a big role in GI spirit boosting, too. While long-legged actresses' pinup pictures adorned footlockers, planes and ships, entertainers brought many hours of laughter to overseas troops in person. Show-biz people performed for our Armed Forces under the din of artillery fire. Many on-screen heroes did their part by joining the military for real.

We children also participated in the war effort. We used our allowances to buy defense stamps and bonds in our schools. We helped collect metal, newspapers and worn-out tires. Boy and Girl Scout troops and other youth organizations headed many of these scrap drives.

To promote recycling, we gathered masses of aluminum foil from cigarette and gum packages and other sources and rolled it into large balls. We bundled flattened tin cans from which we had removed the labels and ends. Neighborhoods pushed together as children became home-front war heroes.

Although dauntless in our efforts, we still faced daily lives filled with major inconveniences because of defense needs. Shortages and rationing frustrated civilians who were forced to greatly alter their lifestyles to comply with war demands.

Food ration stamps limited individual consumption of items like sugar, butter, coffee, meat and canned goods, and they had to be used within a certain time period to prevent hoarding. Many people grumbled when their grocery bags couldn't always be filled with the items they

ROSIE THE RIVETER

wanted. "Don't you know there's a war on?" storekeepers retorted.

Gas stations frequently were forced to display "Sorry, No Gas" signs on their pumps to comply with the fuel curtailment. Coping with this restriction was difficult. To deal with the situation, the government imposed a nationwide speed limit of 35 miles per hour and assigned gas coupons to motorists. Our automobile windshields exhibited stickers bearing the letter A, B, C or E. These stickers determined the amount of gasoline each driver was allotted per week. Our driving habits—whether we drove mostly for pleasure, for work or for emergency causes—were considered when determining individual fuel allowances.

Many of us were accustomed to home deliveries of dairy products and baked goods. To lighten the burden of "doing without," some businesses switched to horse-drawn wagons to deliver milk and bread.

The scarcity of rubber left many children shivering without boots. Inadequate supplies of heating fuel left some families shivering in cold houses. We also lacked paper products, shoes, nylon stockings, batteries and even cotton to manufacture babies' diapers.

In despair, some people turned to the black market to obtain scarce items. Although a variety of rationed articles were available through this illegal outlet, meat and fuel seemed to be the top sellers. But buying from the black market usually meant paying higher prices.

Zoos, public parks, rooftops and especially family back yards became the homes of millions of "victory gardens." Americans dug into the earth to plant their own food, and in 1943 they produced one-third of the vegetables eaten in the United States.

"Loose Lips Sink Ships" signs hung in public places, blurting out their warning as a precaution against spies. Citizens were cautioned against telling anyone where their serviceman was being sent. Americans no longer enjoyed musical-request shows on radio; they were prohibited because of their potential for transmitting coded messages. The government also banned the broadcast of weather reports for fear that the enemy would use them to plan bombing raids.

Still devastated by the attack on Pearl Harbor, we feared an enemy assault on the mainland. This apprehension prompted millions to volunteer as home-front air-raid wardens. Wearing their identifying armbands, wardens often had a difficult time getting the public to take air-raid drills seriously. Even as the piercing alarm cut into the night, wardens frequently met with resistance as they whisked people off the streets and into their homes. When they spied rays of light leaking out into the darkness, wardens banged on the doors of offending homes, stores and offices, shouting, "Lights off!"

Posters bearing a picture of Uncle Sam and the slogan "I Want You for the U.S. Army—Enlist Now" peppered buses, store windows and public buildings. Women who stayed at home tearfully sang songs such as *I'll Keep the Love Light Burning, Now Is the Hour* and *I'll Walk Alone* for their absent GIs.

With a smile on her face and a prayer in her heart, the American mom sent her son into military service. Male draftees of mixed ages from all corners of the nation and every walk of life were proud to fight for our country as they marched off to war with the strains of Irving Berlin's *This Is the Army, Mr. Jones!* ringing in their ears.

Mothers sent letters and packages filled with memories of home to their fighting offspring. Small flags bearing a blue star hung in living-room windows, each star representing a son in the Armed Forces. A flag bearing a gold star meant a mother had lost her boy to the enemy. Many flags held more than one star.

While millions became "Government Issue," or GIs, many men refused to be drafted because of religious beliefs and chose prison rather than armed service. Others who wanted to fight were exempted from the service, classified "4-F" because of physical or mental impairment. Discontented, these men wanted to do their duty, and they served their country by protecting the people back home as members of the Civil Defense.

V-J Day—that day in 1945 when the war finally burned itself out—meant the end of four troubled years of American history. Americans on the home front had done without, and many had lost loved ones even as we made every effort to help our fighting men win the war. In the process, we had shared a bond of togetherness.

With overwrought emotions, we all celebrated peace with merrymaking, dancing in the streets and prayers of thanksgiving. ★

A Letter From Laura

By William Jones

Childhood during the years of World War II was somewhat restricted and quiet by 21st century standards. Gasoline rationing meant few trips far from home, the fear of infantile paralysis—later known as polio—meant that during summer most public places, from the swimming pool to the ice cream parlor, were closed to children. Even such children's delights as Lionel trains, bicycles and coaster wagons were hard to come by.

As a youngster of six in the first grade living near Princeton, N.J., there was, however, one wonderful resource largely unaffected by the war: our town's public library.

Friday evening or Saturday afternoon invariably brought a weekly shopping trip to town and while father was in the A&P Grocery, mother headed for the library. The Princeton library was in what appeared to be an old house with the books spread throughout the rooms with one devoted to the children's collection.

I early discovered such future classics as *Mike Mulligan and His Steamshovel* by Virginia Lee Burton, *The Wonderful Locomotive* by Cornelia Meigs and *Horton Hatches the Egg* from the zany world of Dr. Seuss.

But then one Friday evening the children's librarian asked if we like books about pioneer life and she handed us a copy of *Little House in the Big Woods* by Laura Ingalls Wilder.

Just as today's readers become intrigued with the adventures of the Ingalls family, we were smitten. Mother settled into the habit of reading aloud a chapter or two each evening. We soon knew the Ingalls family and then met Almanzo Wilder and the adventures continued.

Mother in conversation one day wondered about what Laura might be doing now, and what had become of the other characters in the stories. The questions seemed to increase until Mother one day proposed we write a letter to Laura. After much discussion it was prepared and sent in care of the publisher. We had plenty of nagging doubts that it would be received by Mrs. Wilder or that she would care to reply.

Then one day several weeks later it appeared in our post office box—a letter from Laura!

Here is the text of her letter to my mother:

Laura and Almanzo as a young married couple, circa 1885. Photo courtesy Laura Ingalls Wilder Home Association, Mansfield, Mo.

Rocky Ridge Farm
Mansfield, Missouri
June 27, 1944

Dear Mrs. Jones,

It was a pleasure to have your letter, but I have been so busy with the last of house-cleaning and company that I have been slow in answering. I do all my own work and an eleven room house takes some doing.

I am so glad you like my books and that you think them a good influence for children.

You are right in thinking I am the Laura of the books, which are altogether my memories.

These Happy Golden Years is the last book I expect to write, though there are many stories in the years that followed.

But I will answer some of your questions.

We have one child, our daughter Rose, born in the little house. You may know of her—

Rose Wilder Lane. She is a writer of short stories, books and magazine articles. Her home is in Connecticut. She has no children so I am not a grandmother. Carrie and Grace married but had no children.

Sister Carrie and I are the only ones of our family now living. Mary never recovered her sight and did not marry.

DeSmet is a large, very modern town now, but we left there nearly fifty years ago and have lived here ever since.

I have worn my hair short for a good many years, tailored cut in the back and long enough in front to curl and fluff around my face. No permanents, just a home made curl.

I never smoked nor drank nor do I wear any skirts so short as the fashion is. Do not paint my finger nails nor use rouge, just keep my complexion good and powder lightly. My hair is perfectly white. By no stretch of imagination could I ever have been called ultra-modern. My wedding ring was a medium wide, plain gold band.

Almanzo and I live by ourselves on our farm, but we do not farm now. The farm at one time was 200 acres and we kept a herd of cows, mostly Jerseys. Also we kept a flock of 300 leghorn hens which were my especial care. And always we had fine horses.

Now we have only three milk goats— Saanens. We have sold the land until we have only 75 acres with the old farm house.

The land is all meadow, pasture and timber, for Almanzo is 87 years old and I am 77, not able to do much work now, glad and thankful we are still able to care for ourselves and each other.

I thank you for your kind letter and hope I have not bored you with my reply.

Yours sincerely,
Laura Ingalls Wilder

P.S. We have no horses now. Drive a Chrysler car instead.

Almost exactly a decade later I was in high school, the family had moved to Denver shortly after the war and my younger sister Kathy was about to be introduced to the *Little House* books. From time to time I listened in as Mother read to her and we discussed the treasured letter from Laura received years earlier.

The idea arose of writing another letter to Laura. We knew she must be elderly by now, but decided to try. This time we mailed it directly to her home in Mansfield, Mo.

Again sever weeks passed. Then, to our surprise and delight, another letter from Laura arrived.

It brought the sad news of Almanzo's passing, but clearly Laura was still active for a woman of 87. We were thrilled to have continued our special link to her.

I thank you for the kind things you say of my books and hope your little girls will like my stories. Love to you both.

Your friend,
Laura Ingalls Wilder
P.S. I agree with you that children today have so much they become bored with everything. Children were better off in the old days when they had less.—L.I.W.

In less than three years Laura died at the age of 90 on Feb. 10, 1957.

Along with millions of her other readers, we were saddened by news of her passing, but treasured our personal messages from Laura and the world of the "Little House."

Years later I shared the letters with my daughter Courtney after she had been introduced to Laura through the books. In our age of computers, boys and girls somehow continue to be intrigued and inspired by these stories that bring alive the spirit of pioneer America. ✫

Laura (Ingalls) and Almanzo Wilder on the grounds of their Mansfield farm in 1942, not long before Almanzo's death. Photo courtesy Laura Ingalls Wilder Home Association, Mansfield, Mo.

Here is what she wrote in her abbreviated second letter.

Mansfield, Mo.
August 17th 1954

Dear Mrs. Jones,

It is interesting to hear from you again after many years. How time does fly!

Mr. Wilder—Almanzo—died October 23, 1949. I am now 87 years old and living by myself in the home where I was when I wrote you in 1944.

Our only child, Rose Wilder Lane, lives in Connecticut.

Laura's desk. Photo courtesy Laura Ingalls Wilder Home Association, Mansfield, Mo.

Mrs. George Jones
3469 W. Hayward Pl.
Denver

Mansfield, Mo,
August 17th 1954

Dear Mrs Jones,
    It is interesting to hear from you again after many years.
How time does fly!
    Mr Wilder, Almanzo, died October 23, 1949. I am now 87 years old and living by myself in the home where I was when I wrote to you in 1944.
    Our only child, Rose Wilder Lane, lives in Connecticut.
    I thank you for the kind things you say of my books and hope your little girl will like my stories.
    Love to you both.
        Your friend
        Laura Ingalls Wilder.

P. S. I agree with you that children to day have so much they become bored with everything. Children were better off in the old days when they had less.

            L. I. W.